The Panic Diaries

The Panic Diaries

*The truth about panic attacks
and how to survive them*

Jeanne Jordan and Julie Pedersen, PhD

A GODSFIELD BOOK
www.godsfieldpress.com

First published in Great Britain in 2005 by Godsfield Press,
a division of Octopus Publishing Group Ltd
2–4 Heron Quays
Docklands
London E14 4JP

1 3 5 7 9 10 8 6 4 2

Printed and bound in England

ISBN 1 84181 283 8
EAN 9781841812830

The authors have made every effort to trace copyright owners. Where they
have failed, they offer their apologies and undertake to make proper
acknowledgement where possible in reprints.

This book has been written and published strictly for informational purposes,
and in no way should it be used as a substitute for consultation with your
medical doctor or health care professional. All facts in this book came from
medical files, clinical journals, scientific publications, personal interviews,
published trade books, self-published materials by experts, magazine articles
and the personal-practice experiences of the authorities quoted or sources
cited. You should not consider educational material herein to be the practice
of medicine or to replace consultation with a physician or other medical
practitioner. The author and publisher are providing you with information in
this work so that you can have the knowledge and can choose, at your own
risk, to act on that knowledge.

CONTENTS

ACKNOWLEDGEMENTS

We would like to thank our families for their patience and untold support while we wrote this book. We'd also like to thank Dr Charles Stevens and Dr Mark Hantoot for the time and effort they gave to this project as well as our Editor, Brenda Rosen, whose encouraging words kept us going. Finally, we'd like to thank all the contributors who bravely shared their personal stories with us. Namaste.

INTRODUCTION

———————

WHAT KEPT EMILY DICKINSON locked inside her Massachusetts home for the final ten years of her life? What caused Sigmund Freud, the father of psychoanalytic theory, to faint at the prospect of boarding a train in Vienna? What compelled us to write this book?

The simple answer is panic.

But panic is anything but simple. Panic is a complex physical, psychological, neurological, social and cultural phenomenon. Yikes! In other words, panic is a *big* thing. It's not easy to describe. It's not easy to define. And it's certainly not easy to live with.

But many people do live with it every day. People you'd least expect, like the famed naturalist and author Charles Darwin, who wrote in his journal that he was tortured by 'a sensation of fear ... accompanied by a troubled beating of the heart, sweat, trembling of muscles'. These symptoms baffled his physicians. Today, he would most likely be diagnosed with panic disorder aggravated by agoraphobia.[1]

Darwin wasn't alone. The list of people who have suffered from panic and related anxiety disorders reads like a *Who's Who*: Alfred Lord Tennyson, Abraham Lincoln and Isaac Newton; poets, presidents and scientists; celebrities, broadcasters, doctors, lawyers and CEOs – they've all been in the ring and wrestled with the wicked beast of panic. We've been there, too – along with those individuals whose stories appear in this book and approximately two hundred million other people around the world. That's a lot of people. And those are just the ones we know about – the ones who have spoken up or gone to a doctor, so that the people who gather statistics about this sort of thing could estimate that more than 3 per cent of the world's population suffers from panic or some form of anxiety disorder.[2] But not everybody who suffers seeks help. The stigma of anxiety and panic prevents many people from taking that first step, so the actual percentage could be much higher. There could be a silent epidemic.

Why silent? Because it's one thing to talk to a doctor, psychiatrist or psychologist about your symptoms, but just try to explain your panic attack to someone who has never experienced one, like your spouse or your boss or your best friend. Either they'll recommend the sure-fire cure that worked for Aunt Ruby or they'll just stare and ask you that question – that dreaded, horrible, awful question – 'What are you afraid of?'

Fear. The basic building block of panic. Now fear itself isn't a bad thing. It's a necessary thing, hard-wired into our biology in the 'fight or flight' response. If not for this response, many of our ancestors would have been gobbled up by sabre-toothed tigers or trampled by woolly mammoths. While we don't have to worry much about wild beasts any more, there are plenty of real threats and dangers lurking in our midst, from terrorist threats to the echo of footsteps behind you in a dark carpark. When we're faced with one of these situations, our fight or flight mechanism kicks in and we either fight or fly. That's basically what happens during a panic attack, with one key difference. The threat – the danger or the horrible thing that might happen – is not outside, in the world. It's inside, in the world of the mind.

Funny thing about the mind, if it 'thinks' there's a danger, it sounds an alarm and the body responds as if there were a 'real' danger. Once the body receives the alarm signal from the brain, once that mechanism kicks in, you're off and running; you're fighting or fleeing. Now it's one thing to fight or fly when a woolly mammoth is chasing you through a prehistoric forest. But it's another matter entirely when you're sitting in a restaurant across from your significant other sipping Chianti when your flight mechanism kicks in.

Fear of woolly mammoths is completely understandable; it's what we'd call a normal or rational fear. But fear of ... the restaurant? The waiter? The Chianti? These fears would generally be considered abnormal (unless, of course, there's a bomb in the restaurant, or your waiter's packing a pistol, or there's arsenic in your wine). But for the purposes of this book, let's assume that the restaurant, the waiter and the Chianti are all harmless. Let's assume that what you're responding to is an *imagined danger*.

Imagined. Not real. So if it's *not real*, why have two hundred million people felt the adrenalin pumping through their veins in similar situations?

Funny thing about the body, it can't tell the difference between 'real' and 'imagined'. All the body knows is that it received a signal from the brain and the signal is real enough. It starts your heart beating like a jackhammer. It sends your blood pressure plummeting or spiking through the roof. It makes you faint or hyperventilate. It makes you sweat or shake or vomit. Sweating is real. Shaking is real. And vomiting is definitely real.

All of this when there's no real threat. Well, the threat may not be real, but the fear certainly is, which brings us back to the 'why' of it. Why are we afraid? Why do we have panic attacks? The truth is that no one knows. But there are theories, lots and lots of theories.

Many psychiatrists and physicians would argue that it all comes down to the chemistry of the brain, that 1.5 kilo collection of 100,000,000,000,000 neural connections synapsing inside the skull. That's one hundred trillion connections. That's a lot of circuitry and a lot of wiring. It's easy to see how something could go wrong.

But we're not just brains in vats. Our brains are embedded in our bodies and our bodies are embedded in a world, the real physical world that we walk around in every day. In this world we experience many difficult things, among them stress and fear and pain, along with some terrific things, like joy and love and laughter. All of these things together make us who we are. Perhaps panic is just part of the human condition, a phenomenon that arises out of the complex interactions between our brains, our bodies and the world.

Then again, panic could be something else altogether, such as a result of the frenetic pace of the world we live in today. We're pulled in all directions, subjecting our human bodies to a degree of stress they simply weren't made to handle: working 60 hours a week; caring for a house, children, and ageing parents; paying for that big car and that bigger house with its state-of-the-art kitchen that we never eat in anyway.

So, how long have humans suffered from panic? Hundreds of years? Thousands of years? What about Adam and Eve? Did they have panic attacks (we mean before the whole apple thing) back when paradise was paradise? It's hard to say. One thing is certain, though. We don't live in paradise any more. We live in a global village where news of disaster spreads faster than wildfire. We live in a world of perpetual 'duck and cover', a world of terror alerts scrolling across the bottom of our television screens. A world where the evening news feeds our fear with stories of how window blinds can kill, how escalators can maim, or how the daily aspirin that's good for your heart may be destroying your pancreas.

Could that be why millions of people are struggling with panic today? We think that might be a piece of the panic puzzle. But as we've said, panic is a complex phenomenon. It's a story that begins at the start of Western culture, when the Greek god Pan first descended from the sky. And yet, panic is not strictly a Western disease. It cuts across all cultures. Malaysian women suffer from *latah*, or 'hyper-startle syndrome'. Inuits suffer from a disorder known as 'kayak angst', a condition that makes them afraid to venture outdoors. It's a story that's still unfolding, playing itself out in the lives of the millions of people around the world who struggle with panic and other anxiety-related disorders every day.

We're two of those people. Journalists by trade, we wanted to get the facts and tell the whole story, so we dug up everything we could find, from Greek mythology to cutting-edge technology. Then we talked to people – people we know, as well as virtual strangers – and asked them to share personal stories of panic with us. In the following pages you'll read their stories as well as some of our own. You'll learn what panic attacks are and what they are not. You'll learn the history of panic, the causes of panic and treatment options for panic attacks. In the last chapter, we'll tell you what worked for us ... and what didn't.

You may have already noticed that we've written this book in a somewhat whimsical voice. We'd like you to know that this was done strictly for medicinal purposes. Humour is some of the best medicine out there. The truth is you can't laugh (we mean a hearty belly laugh) and feel anxious at the same moment.[3] Laughing can reduce your blood pressure and your heart rate.[4] It can fight disease by boosting your white blood cells. It can reduce symptoms of fatigue, depression and anxiety. It can enhance your memory and improve your problem solving skills. It can increase your income by 40 per cent (okay, we're just kidding about the income, but it can be a great therapeutic tool). And developing your capacity for humour can eventually help you to recognize the humour in almost any situation.

That's why we decided to make this book entertaining as well as informative. We're not saying that you'll be rolling off your chair, laughing and gasping for air at every turn of the page. We *are* saying that humour can counter the anxiety and stress of some very serious stuff. As the comedian Bill Cosby once said, 'If you can laugh at it, you can survive it.'

But life is about more than just survival. Life is about feeling good.

If you've been struggling with panic, don't despair. You can feel good again. Maybe not today or tomorrow, but with hard work and a little time, it definitely can happen.

1 THE BIG BAD WOLF

I have a dragon to slay in my soul. But I don't know what it is.[5]

BILLY BOB THORNTON, ACTOR

ONCE UPON A TIME there was a Greek god named Pan. According to mythological records, Pan was half goat and half man – you can guess which half. It is said that he had the head, chest and arms of a man and the legs, horns and ears of a goat. You might say he wasn't much to look at. Apparently the nurse in the mythological delivery room agreed. The moment she saw this tiny infant with horns and goat ears and a beard, she was filled with terror and ran from the room screaming.

Which brings us to the word 'panic'. *Panic* is derived from the name of the Greek god Pan, but not simply because he was an ugly baby. Plenty of babies are, well... less than beautiful. But they grow and change. Not Pan. He scared the daylights out of the first person who ever laid eyes on him and he kept it up all his life.

Pan was the god of woods and fields. He was also the god of goats, sheep, and shepherds. He was a busy guy. But the majority of his time was spent 'ruling over the forests', which basically meant scaring forest travellers half to death.

We say 'forest travellers' because not only mere mortals traipsed through the woods back then. Nymphs and sirens frolicked; soldiers and hunters fought and hunted; woodsmen and messengers passed through the forests on business. Other creatures tarried there, too. Evidently, if you had to get from here to there, you had to go through the woods, and if you went through the woods, there was a good chance you would encounter Pan. The rumour was that Pan would descend out of the blue to terrify those forest travellers.

Now, it seems that Pan had a bit of a crush on a nymph called Syrinx. (Well, crush might be a little romantic for what Pan was feeling.) One night, as Syrinx was frolicking along the river, Pan called out to her in that oh-so-sexy man-goat voice of his. Of course, Syrinx did what any self-respecting nymph would do – she froze in terror.

Pan smiled, certain that he had captured his little nymph. But it was not to be, for as Pan approached the frozen Syrinx, her good buddies – the river nymphs – transformed her into reeds. This really annoyed Pan, so he tore the reeds from the shore and squeezed them together, creating the musical instrument we know today as the pan pipes. From then on, all Pan had to do was to blow into the pipes and the sound of it echoing through the forests would scare travellers half to death.

It's not hard to imagine feeling frightened in a dark forest. No wonder the Grimm brothers placed so many of their fairy-tale children in the mysterious darkness of the woods: Little Red Riding Hood, Hansel and Gretel, Snow White ... kids and monsters – nothing new there. But kids and panic? Let's take a closer look.

Panic diary
Jeanne at age seven
6 April 1963

Dear Diary,

I'm seven years old, sitting at a wooden desk, clutching my fat pencil and writing neatly on the dotted line. Sister Mary Louise calls out the next spelling word. I bend over the paper, pencil poised, when I feel it. It's there, deep in my belly. First it's just cold, like an ice cube sitting in my tummy, but then it moves, rumbles up to my chest, pushes at my throat. This is my monster.

I open my mouth and try to pull in air, try to push the monster back down, but it's strong, stronger than me, I think. I look at the big clock on the wall. Four minutes until the lunch bell. Four long minutes. Sister Mary Louise says another spelling word. The monster is pushing hard against my throat. It's choking me.

I set down my pencil. Rub my little palms together and take one deep breath after another. I can't sit here any more. I have to run. But I won't, because it's against the rules. I squirm in my seat. Sister Mary Louise frowns at me: the troublemaker. She calls out another word. I pick up my pencil. Roll it in my hands. Look again at the clock. Two more minutes. She says the last word.

I look around at all the class bent over their papers. I want to be like them. I try to write, but I can't remember the word Sister just said. I stare at the four empty lines on my paper. I'm a good speller, but I'm going to get a low mark again. Sister says, 'Pass your papers forward.' Everyone will see my empty spaces.

We all stand and walk slowly and quietly to the cloakroom for our lunches. I want to bolt from the line and run out of the door, but I make my legs take small steps. We walk silently, single file down the stairs to the dining hall. As soon as we push through the heavy doors, it's loud. Hundreds of children sit at long tables, eating, talking and laughing. The monster in my belly doesn't like loud. I can pull in air now. I can push the monster back down. For a while, anyway.

HISTORY'S 'BELIEVE IT OR NOT' PANIC MUSEUM

The 1960s were not a good time to have a childhood mental health crisis – or any kind of mental health crisis, for that matter. Back then there was no such thing as panic disorder. No such thing as a panic attack. Not for kids, and not for adults. Back then, if you were seven years old and had a monster in your belly, you were probably 'spoiled' or 'difficult' or 'nervous'. And if you were an adult in the 1960s – an adult frozen with fear in the soup aisle of the supermarket – you weren't having a panic attack, you were suffering from 'anxiety neurosis'.

Anxiety neurosis. Now there's a term you'd rather not have plastered on your CV. Let's see what it means.

Anxiety: a painful sense of unease in the mind. From the Latin *angere*, which means 'to trouble' or 'to choke'.

Neurosis: a disorder characterized by anxiety, compulsions, fear and depression.

They just tossed it all together back then, sort of a catch-all for anything that ailed you. Still, this is better than what would have happened a hundred years ago when a young doctor named Sigmund Freud (1856–1939) began wandering through the uncharted territory of the human psyche.

Imagine yourself in Vienna, minding your own business, shopping for a little schnitzel, when out of the blue, your heart starts pounding in your chest. You start sweating. You feel a choking sensation. You're dizzy, you can hardly see the butcher across the counter, and you're certain – absolutely certain – that you're about to die.

If you were fortunate enough to have heard of this young Dr Freud, you might have found yourself on his couch, telling him about the whole schnitzel thing. But that's where your luck would have ended, because back then, your little schnitzel episode would not have been diagnosed as a panic attack. It would have been attributed – after many more visits to the couch – to an envy (you know the one we're talking about) or a complex (lots to choose from here), or a subconscious urge, or a repressed desire, or even a libidinous lust for the butcher. And you thought you were just shopping for schnitzel! Who knew you wanted to sleep with Herr Wurstmann?

And before that? What labels may have been slapped on someone with panic or anxiety disorders two hundred or five hundred or even a thousand years ago? If you were lucky, you might have been hailed as a prophet or a visionary, or even a seer or a saint. On the other hand, you could have been treated with leeches, burnt at the stake, tossed in an asylum, or even accused of heresy or treason.

It wouldn't be the last time in history that someone failed to make a correct diagnosis. As recently as a hundred years ago, 10 to 15 per cent of all institutionalized psychiatric patients were diagnosed with a fatal disease called *general paresis of the insane*. This disease included symptoms of mania, delusion, incoherence, paralysis, and ultimately death. For years, these people were considered just plain nuts. Then the field of microbiology opened up. Guess what? It turns out that all those people suffering from *general paresis of the insane* were actually suffering from a brain infection caused by *Treponema pallidum*, the micro-organism that causes syphilis.

Talk about one of those 'good news/bad news' moments: 'Darling, I went to the doctor today and it turns out I'm not insane....'

WE'VE COME A LONG WAY, BABY

But that was then and this is now. If you happen to suffer from panic attacks or anxiety disorders, the truth is, you couldn't have picked a better time to be born. We've come a long way from the Dark Ages of the mind and a long way from the 1960s. If you want to think of it in astronomical terms, you might say we're in the Big Bang moment, or in that third or fourth millisecond after the Big Bang. You might say that we're at the dawn of a new age, a veritable Renaissance or Enlightenment.

Okay, maybe that's overstating things a bit, but medical professionals today do have a more secure foothold in understanding and treating panic and anxiety disorders. What's changed? What's so different between these days and the days of the 1960s? Or the 1660s? Or the 960s?

Personally, we think it has a lot to do with indoor plumbing.

But one of the biggest changes came about in 1980. That's the year the 'new and improved' version of a big black book called the DSM was published. (Actually, it's a big grey book, but we thought 'big black book' sounded better.) The DSM, also known as the *Diagnostic and Statistical Manual of Mental Disorders*, or as we like to call it, *Ye Olde DSM*, is published by the American Psychiatric Association. It's an important book, almost a thousand pages long, filled with descriptions and statistics and symptoms of hundreds of mental disorders.

It is *the* book on mental illness and is often described as 'The Bible of Psychiatry'. Used around the world as a diagnostic guide, it has been translated into more than 6,000 languages. (Okay, it was only 22 languages, but still, that's a lot.)

Prior to 1980, the DSM was in a shambles. Psychiatrists, psychologists and psychoanalysts had no consistent way of distinguishing between the many and varied anxiety-related mental illnesses. You might say there was a bit of a diagnostic crisis going on. Since proper diagnosis is the key to effective treatment, missing the diagnosis results in incorrect treatment.

Thank goodness for a psychiatrist by the name of Robert Spitzer. In 1974, this ambitious young doctor from Columbia University took on the task of cleaning up the DSM. This was fine with other psychiatrists, few of whom imagined that Spitzer's work would yield anything useful.

In a 2003 interview, Spitzer reflected back on this time in his life. 'Nobody worried very much about what direction it was going to take, I guess because nobody expected anything ... that was going to be very revolutionary.'[6] As head of the task force to revise the DSM, Spitzer pulled together a team of radical psychiatrists. 'Mavericks,' he called them, 'who represented a different kind of psychiatry than was ... the mainstream at that time.'[7]

For the next six years, Spitzer and his team worked like a group of anthropologists from Mars. They sorted through every scrap of paper, every observation, statistic, and theory – all in an effort to name, classify, clarify and define an array of mental disorders that had previously been in the box labelled 'anxiety neurosis'. It got downright hectic at times, this bunch of guys (and a few girls) crammed into a little room and sometimes shouting at each other, but eventually they got the job done. Under Spitzer's direction, anxiety disorders that had been previously lumped together finally received their own names, including:

- panic disorder
- post-traumatic stress disorder
- agoraphobia
- social phobia
- generalized anxiety disorder

Along with these new names came new treatment options. Psychoanalysis, the talk therapy based on the theories of Sigmund Freud, was no longer the only option. As a matter of fact, it was no longer the treatment of choice.

The DSM has been updated every few years and more anxiety disorders have been added, including:[8]

- obsessive-compulsive disorder
- specific phobia
- acute stress disorder
- substance-induced anxiety disorder
- panic disorder with agoraphobia
- panic disorder without agoraphobia

Today each of these disorders is considered a specific anxiety disorder. However, it is not uncommon for someone to experience overlapping symptoms or symptoms of more than one disorder. For example, someone with agoraphobia might also display symptoms of obsessive-compulsive disorder. Here's where it gets a little tricky: to include both agoraphobia and obsessive-compulsive disorder would be a 'dual diagnosis' and such diagnoses are frowned upon in the medical community. Number one, a dual diagnosis makes it more difficult to treat a patient. Number two, this type of diagnosis is less precise, which means the medical provider is less likely to target the primary disease.

Most psychiatrists and psychologists strive to make a 'differential diagnosis' when it comes to anxiety disorders. That means they want to pick the primary disorder and use it as the basis for treatment. Keep in mind that these disorders are just names and labels: convenient, shorthand ways of referring to a group of symptoms.

THE HOUSE THAT PANIC BUILT

You probably noticed that the term 'panic attacks' did not appear on the list of anxiety disorders. No, that was not an oversight. You may be wondering, 'Why not? Isn't there a disorder called *panicus attackus* or something?'

Technically speaking ... no. A panic attack is one *symptom* of an anxiety disorder. A symptom is a condition resulting from disease and often serves to aid in a diagnosis, like the way a sneeze can be the symptom of a cold. You don't sneeze because you have *sneezitis*, you sneeze because you have a cold or an allergy. So, too, with panic attacks. Think of them as the sneezes of anxiety disorders.

But does the word 'symptom' really do a panic attack justice? It doesn't take a rocket scientist to figure out that during a panic attack something big is going on. Exactly what is a panic attack?

Here's what the DSM says:

A **panic attack** is a discrete period in which there is the sudden onset of intense apprehension, fearfulness or terror, often associated with feelings of impending doom.

Ah, now we're getting somewhere. Intense apprehension. Sudden onset. Terror. And our personal favourite – feelings of impending doom.

Panic diary
Julie at age 43
19 April 2001

Dear Diary,

I'm in the supermarket carpark. I'm trying to get out of my car, but the breathing thing is happening again. It's deep and slow, like a patient on a respirator, and I can't seem to alter its pace. It's like someone else is breathing for me. I hope she knows what she's doing. This slow part is only the beginning. It's just getting going now. I'd better hurry, before it's too late.

I step onto the asphalt. I push my legs, one in front of the other, but I feel like I'm walking through clay, as if the air around me were made of heavy clay and it's so hard to push past all of them. But I do. Somehow. And now I'm in the shop.

I grab a shopping trolley and grip the handles. The trolley

offers a momentary anchor, an object to cling to in case one of the trapdoors opens. The breathing is getting worse. Each breath gnaws at me, pulling me like a great tide into the dark world at the edge of fainting, the edge of consciousness.

I'm in the front of the shop, in the fruit section. Other people swoosh past me but they seem a million miles away, as if we're travelling in space and I'm on a different plane where they can't see me. The breathing thing is getting fast now. My thoughts start racing, flying, shooting through my mind. I can barely grab them. 'Where am I? What am I doing? Supermarket. Supermarket. I'm at the supermarket. But why? Why am I here? Dinner. Food. What? Think of something. Think, think, think!'

I look around at the mounds of fruit, but they look hideous and unfamiliar, like things that grow on other planets. Except for the apples. Apples. I push toward the apples. Just a step, but my heart starts smashing against the walls of my chest. Step, smash. Step, smash. I cross the infinite space between the apples and me, all three or four feet of infinite space.

I can hardly breathe now. I feel like I'm slipping outside of myself, as if someone popped the balloon that is me and I'm seeping out into the air. I reach out to grab an apple and my hand is shaking. It looks like someone else's hand. I thrust it quickly inside my pocket. Maybe it will stop shaking. I look up. I try to look at something else, but the shop is so vast, the walls at the end so far away, and now it feels like it's fading. Like the whole world is fading. Like the world is just a picture. A picture drawn in coloured chalk on the pavement and it's just begun to rain. I'd better go before the world disappears. Step, smash. I better go before it's too late. Step, smash.

Whew! That's one heck of a sneeze, one heck of a symptom. Now here's a subtle but important point: sneezes are easy to recognize. If you sneeze, you know it. If someone else sneezes near you, you know it. You can be in a lift with a complete stranger and if they sneeze, it's apparent. We recognize a sneeze as a sneeze and can distinguish it from a hiccup or a cough because sneezes have a set of features or characteristics. However, not every sneeze has every feature. Some sneezes are short and quiet. Others are long and loud. Some have a rhythmic warm-up phase accompanied by a modern version of an ancient chant. Yet, through all this diversity – to quote Gertrude Stein's sister, who was allergic to roses – a sneeze is a sneeze is a sneeze.

And here's another important point: panic attacks are not as easy to recognize as sneezes. You can have a panic attack and think you're having a heart attack. You can know a person very well and not recognize that they're having a panic attack. But, just like sneezes, panic attacks have a set of features and characteristics that distinguish them from other things. Here they are, straight from the DSM:

Criteria for Panic Attack
- palpitations, pounding heart or accelerated heart rate
- sweating
- trembling or shaking
- sensations of shortness of breath or smothering
- feelings of choking
- chest pain or discomfort
- nausea or abdominal distress
- feeling dizzy, unsteady, light-headed or faint
- chills or hot flashes
- paresthesias (numbness or tingling sensation)

- fear of losing control or going crazy
- fear of dying
- derealization (feelings of unreality) or depersonalization (being detached from oneself)

Does every panic attack have every one of these features? No, not usually, and let's thank our lucky stars for that. But it must have at least four of the above features to be considered a panic attack.

Notice that the first ten of these symptoms have a *physical* component. The last three have a *psychological* or *cognitive* component. Most panic attacks have several physical symptoms, but if you do the maths, you'll see that at least one of your symptoms must be physical. If you are walking around with feelings of fear and impending doom but don't have any of the physical symptoms, you are not having panic attacks. What you are experiencing are feelings of fear and impending doom and you should consider a career change, perhaps becoming an existentialist writer or opening a dimly lit café near a well-established university. In any case, fear without physical symptoms is not panic.

Speaking of fear, remember in the introduction when we said that fear was the basic building block of panic? For those of you who didn't read the introduction – go back and read it. It contains subliminal positive messages and post-hypnotic suggestions that are designed to induce a state of calmness and well-being to help you digest the information in this book. Just kidding. Okay, back to fear.

It's reasonable and necessary to be afraid in certain situations so you can do what you must to *get out of danger*, such as when a car is speeding straight for you, a gun is jammed into your ribs, or a grizzly bear is waiting at the edge of the hiking trail. Suddenly your heart is pounding out of your chest, it's hard to breathe, and you're as dizzy as the Fräulein in the Schnitzel Shoppe – but it's okay. It's okay because you really are in danger! Your brain and your body are doing exactly what they're supposed to be doing – giving you the best they've got to get you out of danger.

But what about when you're not in 'real' danger? What about when you're standing in line at your local bank, waiting patiently to deposit your pay cheque, and suddenly you're gripped by terror? Now if the terror is related to your bank balance or if there's a gunman waving a pistol at a clerk, then that's a little different. But let's assume you've got plenty of cash and there's no gun anywhere. There's no real danger, no real threat, but there you are, your heart pounding away, your body and brain giving you the old 'get out of danger' routine.

So, what are you afraid of? There it is, the big question. So big we'll say it again. What are you afraid of?

For most sufferers of panic, or 'panickers' as we'll call ourselves from here on, this can be a tough question to answer. We did a little 'in the trenches' research and here's what we came up with:

Panicker's List of Fears
- losing control
- dying
- going crazy
- having a heart attack
- having a stroke
- getting hurt
- acting inappropriately
- acting on impulse

- fainting
- losing touch with reality
- dissolving into nothingness
- disappearing
- annihilation
- chocolate

Just for the record, we made up the last item on the list. Most people who have panic attacks are not afraid of chocolate. But panic attacks can differ tremendously from person to person, so in theory there may be people who are afraid of chocolate. Unfortunately, there are no chocolate statistics available.

In the next chapters we'll take a closer look at the anxiety disorders we've mentioned above. We'll also take a look at some successful treatments and promising new therapies.

But what we have found is that conquering panic is less about slaying the beast and more about, well, dancing with it. So at the end of each chapter we'll be outlining a few techniques for managing and overcoming panic. Think of these techniques as dance steps, like a tango or a cha-cha, that you'll practise over and over until eventually they become second nature. (Remember, these dance steps are not meant to replace the care of a doctor or therapist.) Now, some of these techniques are a combination of therapies, but most prominently reflect the methods of Dr Claire Weekes, who published her first book on overcoming 'nervous illness' in 1969. She was the first to suggest a mind–body connection in the treatment of anxiety, with methods meant to guide sufferers to the inner strength that they sometimes can't seem to find.

DANCING WITH PANIC: THE PANIC WALTZ

The first step in the panic waltz is breathing. Of course you already know how to breathe, but this is a different type of breathing. It's called abdominal breathing, and it can increase oxygen to your brain, excrete toxins from your body, and stimulate your parasympathetic nervous system, all of which can result in a wonderful state of calm.

Okay, first get comfortable. Sit in a chair or cross-legged on the floor and close your eyes. Now slowly draw a breath in through your nostrils, down to your diaphragm (below your breastbone and above your navel), and exhale through your nostrils.

As you breathe, try to visualize your breath as a white ribbon of energy that travels down to your abdomen, then turns over and follows the same path in reverse as you exhale. This is the panic waltz. Try to do it for five minutes each day. If you can't manage five minutes, do four or even three minutes. Something is better than nothing.

During panic

The great thing about the panic waltz is that it can be done anywhere – in a plane, in a lift, or even in a mythological forest. You don't have to close your eyes if it's not practical. You don't even have to sit down. Just follow the steps as described above. Breathe.

FUN FACTS TO IMPRESS YOUR FRIENDS

- The average age when people suffer a first panic attack is their early twenties
- Panic is a type of grass, of the genus *Panicum*, commonly called Panic Grass

2 A ROSE IS A ROSE IS A THORNY SON OF A ...

It's that feeling when you almost get in a car wreck and you swerve, and for a second there are needles in your head and needles in your body. It's that moment, but stretched out.[9]

WINONA RYDER, ACTOR

P ANIC ATTACKS ARE A SYMPTOM of many different anxiety disorders, and although we'll be giving you scads of information about each of these disorders, we're not medical doctors. You need the help of a professional to diagnose an anxiety disorder, so if you haven't been to a doctor yet, go now. Well, not right this minute, but soon.

Speaking of doctors, we lined up some pretty impressive ones to act as our consultants on this book. The first is Mark Hantoot, MD, a board-certified psychiatrist and Assistant Clinical Professor of Psychiatry and Behavioral Science at the Feinberg School of Medicine at Northwestern University in Chicago, Illinois. 'Dr Mark' (as we refer to him) previously served as the Medical Director of Northwestern Memorial Hospital's Outpatient Treatment Center, where he remains a Staff Psychiatrist and clinical supervisor. He also serves as Director of Medical Services for Trilogy, Inc. and PRN, PsychResourceNet, a community-based provider of behavioural health and allied services in the Chicago area.

Charles Stevens, MD, or 'Dr Charles', is a certified member of the American Board of Internal Medicine and a member of the American College of Physicians. Dr Charles was Chief Medical Resident at Abbott Northwestern Hospital in Minnesota during his medical training. He currently serves on the ICU committee at Lakeview Hospital in Minnesota and is the Department Chair of Internal Medicine at the Stillwater Medical Group.

Not too long ago, people experiencing panic attacks often found themselves caught in a frustrating game of doctor ping-pong. Running back and forth from the cardiologist to the neurologist to the gastroenterologist, and still no diagnosis. Fortunately, that's all begun to change. Many doctors today can diagnose panic attacks as quickly as your first visit. In addition, they'll often perform tests to rule out other medical conditions that can mimic the symptoms of panic. These conditions include mitral-valve prolapse, hypoglycaemia, hypothyroidism, Cushing's syndrome, temporal lobe epilepsy, diabetes, asthma, audiovestibular dysfunction and cardiac arrhythmias, all of which can produce symptoms also associated with panic attacks.

We could tell you all about these different medical conditions, but it's been our personal experience that panickers sometimes need only hear a symptom or two of a disease before they're convinced they're coming down with it. However, there are a few details you should know about, starting with what happens in the body during a panic attack.

THE LOWDOWN ON PANIC ATTACKS

During a panic attack your brain perceives a threat and sends the signal to trigger the fight or flight response. You might think that since there's no real threat, a panic attack is a misfired signal ... Well, you're right! But that is not necessarily a bad thing. Threats pose an immediate problem, and an immediate problem requires immediate action. If we had to stop and think, even for a second or two, our action would be delayed and the sabre-toothed tiger would gobble us up. That's the advantage to having a fight or flight response hard-wired into our biology. It gets you moving right away. And that's exactly what you want it to do.

Let's get down to the nitty-gritty of the whole fight or flight response. We'll start with the autonomic nervous system, or the ANS, which really has two parts to it: the sympathetic nervous system (sounds friendly, doesn't it?), or the SNS; and the parasympathetic nervous system, or the PNS. The ANS takes care of a long list of basic processes like breathing, circulation and maintaining a comfortable body temperature. The SNS, the sympathetic one, is the part of the nervous system that kickstarts the fight or flight response. The PNS relaxes the body after the fight or flight and restores it to a sense of pre-fight or pre-flight calm.

All clear with the nervous system? Good, now let's move to the brain.

There are two structures in the brain that control the fear response. They're called the *amygdala* and the *hippocampus* (don't you love that word? just picture a university with little hippos carrying backpacks). When you're faced with a threat (whether real or imagined), neurons in the amygdala get very excited and send a chemical message to the *hypothalamus*.

The hypothalamus is like the first stretch of road on the highway of fear. The message travels quickly along this road until it reaches the anterior pituitary gland. Once there, the message convinces the pituitary to produce a hormone called ACTH (for those of you who want to know, ACTH is a nickname for adrenocorticotropic hormone). The ACTH runs from the pituitary all the way down to the adrenal gland, which is located on the kidney. There it tells the adrenal gland to produce more hormones and before you know it you've got all sorts of chemicals shooting through your bloodstream. You've got cortisol and catecholamines and norepinephrine, to name a few.

Now your heart begins to beat faster because it has to redirect blood flow to the large muscles in your arms and legs, which you'll be using to fight or flee. Your lungs have to work harder to take in the extra oxygen you need, so you begin to breathe fast, very fast, so fast that you think you might faint. With all this activity your body heats up, so as a safeguard to overheating you start to sweat. Your blood pressure rises to keep up the circulation, which feeds the muscles, which keep your legs running fast and furiously away from the beast. Wow!

So how long can your body keep up this level of activity? Well, about 15 minutes or so is about as long as your body can tolerate the onslaught of these fight or flight chemicals. That's when the PNS kicks in and says, 'Sorry, fellows, somebody made a mistake.' But if there really is a woolly mammoth hot on your trail, or if someone really has a gun to your head, your PNS won't interfere. As long as the danger is real, your PNS will let the SNS run things. But if the triggering of the fight or flight response was an error, your PNS will send out chemicals to counteract the stress hormones and bring them back to safe levels.

Fear is good. It's the basic building block of survival – and the basic building block of panic. But what a double-edged sword! It can save your life and ruin your day.

Panic diary
Bridgette at age 28
5 March 1983

Dear Diary,
My husband, my young son and I went to visit some friends on Saturday morning. We sat around all morning drinking coffee and eating doughnuts: not a good combination for me.

It must have been the buildup of things: I probably had anxiety before that morning. And for a whole week before that, I'd had pain in my left shoulder and discomfort in my whole body. So that morning, after all that sugar and coffee, we got in the car to leave.

We're driving home on Lake Shore Drive and I feel this pain in my left shoulder and I start thinking I'm having a heart attack. I see signs for hospitals, and I keep rubbing my left shoulder, trying to calm myself down. I don't say anything to my husband.

I'm thinking that I must be having a heart attack right now, and how I've had all these warning signs for ever and just ignored them. But I still don't say a word.

We get back to our home and I rush into the bathroom. I look in the mirror and I think to myself, 'This is it, the heart attack.' Then all of a sudden I start to hyperventilate.

I call a neighbour to come and watch my son so we can go to casualty.

> I'm breathing into a bag because I realize I'm hyperventilating and when we get to the hospital, I tell them, 'I think I'm having a heart attack.' They get me into triage real fast. They do an ECG and some blood work to check my oxygen levels. A few hours later, when the tests come back, they tell me my blood oxygen level is excellent. So is my heart. No heart attack. I go home.
>
> Nobody said anything about panic attacks.

So, what causes panic attacks? Is it nature or nurture? For more than a century, this debate has raged on, and still the question remains unanswered. Thousands of traits make you who you are. Some traits are determined by your genes, or by *nature*. Other traits are determined by your childhood environment or by upbringing, called *nurture*. The general consensus among scientists today is that most traits are developed through a combination of nature and nurture. According to the National Institute of Mental Health, nature can influence nurture and nurture can influence nature.[10] Interesting. Let's start at the beginning, with nature.

ALL IN THE FAMILY *OR* THE HEREDITY FACTOR

Heredity. That means you were born with it. Just like those big baby blues, or Aunt Claire's knobby knees, or your strong nose. Not that there's anything wrong with a strong nose.

There are some impressive research results to support the genetic inheritance theory. Take identical twins, for example. Identical twins share the same genetic make-up and several studies have found that if one twin has an anxiety disorder, the probability of the other twin having an anxiety disorder ranges from 33 to 88 per cent, depending on the specific study. However, when the same studies were conducted with fraternal twins, whose genes are not identical, the results were radically different, revealing a probability range up to 38 per cent.[11] Still higher than in the general public, but significantly lower than identical twins. Even more interesting, other research shows that nearly 75 per cent of all panickers have a first-degree biological relative who also experiences panic attacks.[12] So what about nurture?

THE COGNITIVE THEORY *OR* YOU ARE WHAT YOU THINK

A basic definition of *cognitive* is 'how you think'. The Swiss psychologist and sociologist Jean Piaget held the theory that panic attacks may be the result of the way that a person thinks.[13] Cognitive theorists believe that certain people focus on anxiety-provoking thoughts and these thoughts act as triggers, which in turn set off a panic attack. These thoughts are the product of a panicker's distorted ideas about his life and environment. When he looks at a virtually harmless situation, he sees danger.

Research also shows a strong correlation between children who suffer from separation anxiety and being raised by overly protective adults. Perhaps these parents portray the world as so dangerous that the child develops a distorted view of the world.

Behaviour theorists hold a similar view. Behaviourists believe that panic attacks are the result of a conditioning process that happens over a period of time, 'teaching' you how to respond to your fears in a way that results in panic.

So there you have it, nature or nurture. Now let's look at some of the theories that support the nature *and* nurture model.

We'll call the first one the Switch Theory. Think of your brain as a gigantic circuit board and panic as a light switch on the board. Some people are born with this switch on and others are born with it off. If you were born with your switch on, usually one of your parents has the same switch on, and you are more susceptible to anxiety disorders. When your switch is on, you tend to operate in a state of hyperarousal (and not the good kind of arousal, either). Hyperarousal means your nervous reactions to stress are exaggerated; for example, you are easily startled by loud noises or flashing lights.

Or you might have been born with your switch off, and then something happened in your life that flipped your switch on, perhaps abuse or neglect during childhood. These types of trauma can have a biological effect on the brain. One theory suggests that extreme stress can slow the growth of nerve fibres in the brain, resulting in what amounts to faulty circuitry that leaves your switch in the 'on' position.

A recent University of Chicago study has shown that verbal assaults can be as harmful to the brain as physical trauma. Our expert Dr Mark agrees. 'If I were to ... take a functional image of your brain when you were a child, then subject you to ten years of physical or sexual or emotional abuse, then [take] another scan, your brain [would] look different. There [would] be chemical changes in your brain as a result of this trauma.'

Another theory is one we'll call the Awry Theory. This theory suggests that physical trauma to the brain causes multiple systems in the brain to go awry.[14] Trauma may have occurred during the prenatal days of your life, or perhaps a minor problem took place at the time of your birth, for example, a temporary lack of oxygen. Maybe it was that tumble you took off your first bike, or the time you fell out of the neighbour's apple tree.

Unfortunately, there is no test to prove any of these theories – no blood test, no MRI, no X-ray that your doctor can look at and say, 'Yes, just as I thought, panic disorder with agoraphobia.'

So there you have it. Nature or nurture or ... both?

LADIES FIRST ...

According to the National Institute of Mental Health, more than two-thirds of those who suffer from panic attacks are women.[15] Why is that? The answer depends upon whom you ask. It has been suggested that perhaps a woman's delicate nature puts her more at risk for panic attacks and anxiety disorders. Delicate? Hmmph. Let's look at the whole gender issue for a moment, shall we?

Many women today are jugglers (and not the fun kind you see at the circus, either). On an average day most women have a whole set of plates in the air: childcare, housework, cooking, career and sometimes ageing parents to boot. (It's just a phrase; we certainly aren't suggesting the booting of ageing parents!) And sometimes the plates are on fire: high debt, redundancy, infidelity.

Research has suggested that women who struggle with anxiety disorders often share certain characteristics, such as dependency, separation anxiety, low self-esteem and perfectionism, to name a few.[16] Then what about all the other women who are *not* having panic attacks and who grapple with dependency, separation anxiety, low self-esteem and perfectionism, to name a few? Again, no one really knows.

But here's the good news. Someone is finally looking into it. The Anxiety Disorders Association of America hosted a conference in November 2003, 'Woman and Anxiety Disorders: Setting a Research Agenda'. The focus of the conference was to 'assess the current state of knowledge about women and anxiety disorders and develop a call to action to meet research needs'. It's about time!

Right now the study of the brain and human behaviour is growing in leaps and bounds. In 1999 the first White House conference on mental health was held, and for the first time the Office of the Surgeon General recognized the relationship between mental health and physical health. Surgeon General David Satcher, MD, PhD, stated, 'We recognize that the brain is the integrator of thought, emotion, behavior, and health. Indeed, one of the foremost contributions of contemporary mental health research is the extent to which it has mended the destructive split between mental and physical health.'[17]

We agree. For too many years mind and body have been treated independently in the practice of medicine. This is a typically Western idea. Eastern medicine, on the other hand, has recognized the mind and body as one for centuries. We're just catching up.

Okay, if we don't know really what causes panic attacks, what exactly *do* we know about panic attacks?

THE USUAL SUSPECTS

We know that one of the most common diagnoses for people suffering from panic attacks is panic disorder. The criteria for panic disorder are specific and limited. A panic disorder diagnosis requires that your panic attacks are totally unexpected – that, like our mythological friend Pan, they strike out of the blue, with no trigger of any sort. You're just scrambling eggs in your kitchen one Sunday morning and suddenly you're terrified. Now, you've scrambled eggs on Sunday mornings in the same kitchen for ten years with no problem, so it's not the kitchen or the eggs. It's just out of the blue. If this sounds like your experience of panic attacks, then you may have panic disorder.

Could you be more specific?

But many panic attacks don't strike out of the blue. Many panic attacks are linked to places and situations and objects. If you have panic attacks associated with specific triggers, like getting in a lift or being in a plane or seeing a Komodo dragon, then you are said to have a specific phobia. A specific phobia is characterized by 'strong fear and avoidance of one particular type of object or situation'.[18] The fear and avoidance must be strong enough to interfere with your normal life, which means that the fear makes you change the way you ordinarily behave.

Specific phobias are very common. A worldwide study recently conducted in the Netherlands has suggested that specific phobias occur in approximately 10 per cent of the world's population.[19] That's roughly 680,000,000 people. So if you have a specific phobia, you are definitely not alone.

As for the things people are specifically phobic about? Well, there are enough of them to fill an encyclopedia (and we mean that in the literal sense). It's called *The Encyclopedia of Phobias* and it lists everything from snakes, planes and doorknobs to arachibutyrophobia, which is the name given to the fear of peanut butter sticking to the roof of your mouth.

Panic attacks associated with specific phobias occur only in the direct or imminent presence of the feared object. Usually, it's not hard to tell if you have a specific phobia. On the other hand, you may not know you have one until that fateful day.

Panic diary
Mary at age 48
23 October 1994

Dear Diary,

I'd been an A&E nurse in Chicago's inner city for a couple of years and I needed a break, so I took a three-month assignment at a hospital in St Michael's, Maryland. I arrived in Annapolis and was looking forward to the rest of the drive down to St Michael's.

A few miles ahead of me was the Chesapeake Bay Bridge. It's a big bridge, so big that they have special employees who'll drive your car for you if you can't do it yourself. I've lived in Chicago all my life and tackled the Skyway Bridge many times. It's a frightening thing to be on, but anyone who's ever been on it knows that. There'd be something wrong with you if you weren't afraid. But I wasn't afraid of bridges!

Not 30 seconds later my heart starts pounding in my chest. I feel cold and clammy. I'm starting to breathe fast and my vision's closing up. I try to settle myself, open the window, play with the radio stations. I look ahead and all I can see is the huge monstrosity of this bridge. It seems like it's ten miles long. I can barely see the other side.

I feel dizzy now. Maybe I have food poisoning. Maybe I'm getting ill. I'm a nurse. I can figure this out. I'm having a fight or flight reaction, that's it, something's triggered a huge release of adrenalin and it's whacking me out. But what? What could it be? After what seems like 20 minutes, I make it to the other side. I look in my rearview mirror. The mere sight of the bridge makes me nauseous.

> A few weeks later, my eight-year-old nephew came to visit. I had to pick him up in Annapolis. That meant the bridge. I wanted no part of the bridge. I didn't even want to see it. But I had a little boy waiting for me. I barely made it.
>
> I picked an alternate route back to St Michael's. It was a long way back, through Washington, DC, Delaware and Virginia, but I didn't care how many miles I'd have to drive to avoid the bridge. The funny thing is, after an extra two hundred miles, I arrived at a bridge again. All that way, only to find myself back where I started – in front of a bridge that I did not want to cross.

Fear is a little bit like that; it's like finding yourself in front of a bridge that you don't want to cross. But don't fret, especially if you have a specific phobia, because they are extremely treatable. You'll learn all about that in Chapter 7. For now, let's cross a few more bridges of our own.

LOCATION, LOCATION, LOCATION!

Let's say it's a week after the scrambled egg incident, and you've been invited to dinner with friends (what fun!). Your good friend (we'll call him Perry) picks everyone up and you climb into the back seat of his car. You're riding along, chatting and laughing, on the way to that funky new restaurant that serves the chicken kebabs that you love, when suddenly, you can't breathe, you feel like you're choking, your heart's hammering out of your chest.

Now you've had two panic attacks out of the blue. But here's the rub – now you don't want to cook on Sunday mornings any more, and you certainly don't want to get into the back seat of Perry's car any more.

So does that mean that you have a specific phobia of cars or your kitchen? Not exactly (we told you it was a little confusing).

If your first panic attacks were out of the blue and later you developed anxiety about the possibility of having another panic attack in the same place or situation, you would most likely be diagnosed with situationally predisposed panic attacks.

Situationally predisposed panic attacks are panic attacks that are more likely to occur when you're exposed to a specific situation, but they don't always occur. So now you feel anxious about getting into Perry's car, because last time you were in his car you had a panic attack, but you go anyway, and although you are a little anxious you don't actually have a panic attack. Or maybe you do have another panic attack in his car. The point is that specific phobias *always* elicit the response of panic. Situationally predisposed panic *sometimes* elicits the response of panic and is more often a response to a *previous situation* where you experienced a panic attack: in the kitchen, in a car, or maybe at the bank.

Panic diary
Jeanne at age 40
12 February 1997

Dear Diary,
The pay cheque is on the piano. It's been there for days now. I keep hoping my husband will deposit it, but that's my job. It's always been my job. What's so hard about it? You go to the bank, hand it to the clerk and wait. I used to be able to do it.
    I take a deep breath and tell my five-year-old to put on her

coat. It's a four-block drive to the bank, but by the time I get there I can barely breathe. I hold the steering wheel tight, but my hands still shake. That cold fist grips me deep inside my chest and belly. It's pushing and squeezing. I'm choking. Even though it's 22 degrees outside, I drive with the window open. The frigid air stings my skin.

I pull into the drive-through lane. There's a car in front of me. I wait. A car pulls in behind me. I'm trapped. I can't get out. My heart's pounding. I consider getting out of the car and running the four blocks back home. My hand reaches for the door handle just as the car in front of me pulls away.

It's my turn. I pull forward. I fumble with the heavy plastic tube, then finally send off the pay cheque. I wait. I want to press the accelerator to the floor, but I wait. I want to scream out loud, but I wait. I want to be back home, but I wait.

And then I hear the high-pitched hiss that tells me it's almost over, I'm almost done. The fat tube lands in its cradle and I grab it. My hands shake so badly I can barely get it open. My daughter looks up from her doll, sees my tears, my trembling hands. 'Mummy?' I turn and see the fear in her eyes. It shakes me to my core. I hit the accelerator and pull into the traffic.

In my drive, I breathe a sigh. The air is moving through my lungs again. I jump out of the car. The plastic tube from the bank drops from my lap and lands on the cement. I pick it up and toss it into the back seat ... along with the other one. I'll bring them back ... next time.

So what happens when you won't go to the bank any more? What happens when you won't get into Perry's car any more (which he really doesn't understand, because it has a beautiful leather interior)?

AGORAPHOBIA *OR* THE HOUSE WITHOUT DOORS

Believe it or not, that brings us to agoraphobia. That's right, agoraphobia – that greatly misunderstood word. The translation from ancient Greek is 'fear of an open marketplace', but it's *so* much more than that. It's fear of open marketplaces and closed marketplaces. It's fear of cinemas and restaurants and pubs. It's fear of shopping centres, of driving, of being anywhere a panic attack might strike.

Most people don't realize that agoraphobia is a continuum. At the far end is the inability to leave your house or even to leave a room in your house. At the other end is avoidance behaviour. Avoidance behaviour is just what it sounds like: the avoidance of situations where you previously had a panic attack. More than that, it's the avoidance of any place at all from which it might be difficult to escape in the event that you do have a panic attack.

Trouble is, you never know when a panic attack might strike.

Panic diary
Jenna Glatzer at age 23
7 November 1998

Dear Diary,
The silly thing about it is that I barely even drove any more, and when I did, I was certainly not a reckless driver. Panic disorder can do that to you. I was more or less housebound, but I made little trips within the town occasionally. This time, a police officer pulled me over, supposedly for not making a complete stop at a stop sign. I had to appear in court. My panic went on overdrive, even though my father was with me. I sat in a small

courtroom with about ten other ticket fighters. I couldn't breathe. I was supposed to sit there until the judge called me, but as I battled that throat-closing-surely-I'm-about-to-pass-out feeling, there was just no way I could sit there. My father agreed to stay in the courtroom and come and get me when my name was called.

I walked out to the lobby and took a seat, hoping I could talk myself through it. Instead, it got worse. My facial tics took hold, and I rocked myself back and forth and practised deep breathing. It seemed everything I did just backfired until the panic escalated so badly that I no longer just thought everyone was staring at me … they were. I could sense that people around me were afraid I was about to have a seizure, or that I was having a bad drug trip. Of course, that didn't help, and I had to escape.

I just started walking. My knees buckled and I had no sense of where I was going, but I knew I had to get away and be alone. I found a little corner with a window and my body was wracked with one of the worst panic attacks of my life. The world felt unreal and all I wanted was to be in my bed. What was I thinking, trying to do this? My house was safe. This place wasn't. I wasn't ready.

Safety. For those who suffer from panic disorder with agoraphobia, the desire for safety has ironic implications. The more you pursue safety, the smaller your world becomes. We like to refer to it as 'the incredible shrinking world'. Slowly, all of those things that once made up your life, all of those things that you did without a second thought – food shopping, going to the library or the high street – become less and less possible. As Emily Dickinson wrote in one of her poems, 'the missing all prevented me from missing minor things.' Like walking in a park on a beautiful day, or missing bigger things, like attending your five-year-old daughter's school Christmas party. Feeling that you can't possibly stand in that little room beside all the other mums also means you won't be able to accept the gift wrapped in layers of shiny paper and covered with a full roll of Sellotape. You'll never see the joy and pride in your little girl's eyes. There can be casualties in a shrinking world.

But then again, what if your world's not shrinking, and you don't have a specific phobia, and your panic attacks aren't out of the blue? What if your panic attacks are the result of continuous and never-ending worry?

GAD *OR* WORRY-WARTS

Are you a 'what-iffer'? You know the routine: What if my car won't start; what if I lose my job; what if my partner gets ill; what if I have cancer; what if I can't sleep again tonight? Sounds familiar? If it does, you might be suffering from generalized anxiety disorder, or GAD.

With GAD you feel constantly anxious and worried. That's right, all the time, every day. This anxiety can then build to a panic attack. There's no particular trigger – like the lift or Perry's car – that causes the anxiety. It's just an endless stream of negative thoughts spinning through your mind. Any situation, anything you read about or see on the news can start those thoughts spinning. Compare GAD to having a weak immune system, and the slightest germ of thought about something going wrong can jolt you into thinking the worst.

Panic diary
Jesse Jordan at age 22
November 2003

Dear Diary,
GAD is no fun. There is no realization, no event from the past that, once dealt with, will clear it all up. It's not a specific disorder. It is, unfortunately, general. The last time I remember feeling that creeping cold come over my chest, my heart going a bit too fast, was when I first sat down to write this entry. It was one week ago. I had agreed to share some of my memories and sat down at my laptop around eight-thirty at night. Then, all of a sudden, I felt it. The thought of bringing up the things that create the feeling in myself that I hate so much was suddenly weighing very heavily on me.

I didn't want to write about those things, didn't want to rehash them for fear that the same feeling would return, which, of course, it did anyway. I decided this was not the time and poured myself a small glass of wine and watched television for a few hours.

For the next week I tried to think of something witty and touching, something that was funny and not so harsh that the very writing of it would be some sweat-soaked, stomach-clenching act of catharsis. Nothing had come and I was beginning to think of different ways that I could avoid the project. Then, while at work yesterday, a private little ten-minute one-man show played out that drove me back to the laptop.

The night before I had been out with a friend. We were out late, drinking too much and eating pizzas ravenously. I fell asleep with my clothes on and woke up to a screaming alarm that alerted me to a screaming hangover. I drank 304 cups of coffee and headed to work, hoping for a quiet, peaceful day. Around noon, I was on a conference call with a client and a lender. I was trying to straighten out a misunderstanding so that we could move forward with financing when, in the middle of a sentence, I felt it.

Knowing, as I do, the horrendous effects that copious amounts of alcohol and bar food can have on the digestive system, I immediately feared the worst. The other two went on talking as I shifted in my seat and attempted to gauge the damage. Diarrhoea. Panic. This is the real thing. I pushed the mute button on the phone, hemming and hawing, trying to adjust so that I wasn't putting too much pressure straight down, fearful that something would soak through my trousers and dirty the seat.

I was probably only on the phone another minute or two, but it felt like hours and hours. It seemed as if they knew, and were just asking obvious questions because they found it funny to listen to me squirm. I looked at the clock; it was just after noon. I can take my break, I thought. I can run home, shower, change and burn these clothes. I'll only be a little late getting back.

Finally, an agreement was reached and the lender hung up. The client started to say something else, but I cut him off, telling him I had to get to another meeting.

I threw my coat on and jumped up from my seat. I rushed out, my right hand holding my trouser leg at the thigh, pulling it tight so that nothing could drip down onto my sock. I burst out the doors and into the corridor. I pressed the lift button, but then turned and saw the lavatory. I headed for it, not sure I wanted to see the damage down below, but positive that a little emergency clean up would help before the journey home. I walked into the disabled cubicle (feeling as though, at that moment, I needed it), shut the door and dropped my trousers.

Nothing. Not a spot, not a speck. I searched wildly, but it soon became apparent that there was nothing to find. It was then, at that moment, standing in that cubicle with my trousers around my ankles, that I realized something. The part of myself that I've always hated is linked inexorably to that which I love about myself. My overactive imagination and my empathy are the very things that drive my anxiety to its rabid ends. The creativity I apply to my stories, I also apply to my own life, my own worries and fears.

I was smiling. I was feeling for the first time ever a sort of affection for my anxiety. I still understand, of course, that I don't have that affection while in the grips of an anxiety attack. I understand that my brain needs some retraining, that I need to learn to control it a bit better. But it seems much more manageable now. It no longer feels like I'm fighting an enemy, but simply retraining a screwed-up ally. Looking at the issue with a new outlook and clean underpants.

Worrisome, nagging thoughts, thoughts that you really believe, even though they turn out to be without basis, are among the factors that lead to panic attacks for people with GAD. But panic attacks are just one of the symptoms of this disorder; other symptoms include muscle tension, fatigue, insomnia, poor concentration and irritability.

More than half of those diagnosed with GAD first experienced symptoms in childhood or adolescence.[20] Typically GAD runs a fluctuating course, showing up at major life events such as university graduation. Suddenly, your entire life and all its responsibilities loom before you. While everyone's pounding you on the back and shouting their congratulations, you're trying to figure out what the heck you're going to do with the rest of your life.

It's true that most people experience anxiety, fatigue, insomnia and irritability occasionally. However, GAD represents a continuous anxiety and worry affecting your everyday functioning. According to Dr Charles, some of the highest rates of 'self-medicating' he sees are in patients with GAD. 'I would say that many of the alcoholics I treat have general anxiety disorder and they have learned that alcohol will alleviate at least some of those symptoms.'

Understanding your individual panic attacks, because they are individual, and understanding the particular disorder that you might be struggling with are vital steps on the road to recovery. In this chapter, we've looked at five of the anxiety disorders that can cause panic attacks. Just in case we've totally confused you with Perry and the car and the eggs and the Komodo dragon, here's a list of disorders with definitions from the DSM.

Panic Disorder is characterized by recurrent unexpected panic attacks about which there is persistent concern.

Specific Phobia is characterized by clinically significant anxiety provoked by exposure to a specific feared object or situation, often leading to avoidance behaviour.

Agoraphobia is anxiety about, or avoidance of, places or situations from which escape might be difficult (or embarrassing) or in which help may not be available in the event of having a panic attack or panic-like symptoms.

Panic Disorder with Agoraphobia is characterized by both recurrent unexpected panic attacks and agoraphobia.

Generalized Anxiety Disorder is characterized by at least six months of persistent and excessive anxiety and worry.

So there you have it, five of the 11 disorders in which panic attacks occur. That leaves six to go, and yes, we'll get to them in the following chapters. But first ... shall we dance?

DANCING WITH PANIC: THE FOXTROT

The first step in the panic foxtrot is to turn towards your panic. Yeah, we know it's not as easy as it sounds. The impulse to turn and foxtrot away from panic is primal, but as you've probably noticed, running from your fear just doesn't work. Your fear and your panic are a part of who you are. So take a dance step towards it, or maybe two.

It doesn't matter what your fear is. Whether you're afraid that your heart will stop beating or that you'll go crazy or humiliate yourself, or even if it's all of the above, it doesn't matter. Whatever your fear is, you need to acknowledge it and turn towards it. Remember to talk to your doctor before applying this technique or practising any dance steps.

During a panic attack

Start with the panic waltz. Feel the breath move slowly. Now, turn towards your panic. Look it in the eye, but not in a confrontational manner, simply face it. You understand what it is. You understand that it's temporary and that one day it won't affect you in this way.

MORE FUN FACTS TO IMPRESS YOUR FRIENDS

- About 25 per cent of chest pain patients admitted to hospital emergency departments are diagnosed with panic attacks
- 10 to 15 per cent of the population will have a panic attack at one time in their lives
- Approximately 20 per cent of adult phobias vanish on their own
- Approximately 80 per cent of panic disorder patients experienced an unusually stressful life event not long before their first panic attack

3 WASH YOUR HANDS BEFORE DINNER ... BUT ONLY ONCE!

*I cut my banana into seven slices every morning before
I put it on my cereal.*[21]
WOODY ALLEN, ACTOR AND DIRECTOR

OBSESSIVE-COMPULSIVE DISORDER, or OCD, and social phobia are two more fascinating additions to our complete coverage of the anxiety disorders. OCD is perhaps one of the most misunderstood of the disorders, due primarily to its portrayal on television and in films, where OCD is often characterized by 'crazy' ritualistic behaviours, like counting or washing or stepping over cracks in the pavement. Social phobia, on the other hand, is probably the least talked about of the anxiety disorders.

Both OCD and social phobia can toss you right into the heart of a panic attack. As Dr Mark is quick to remind us, 'Panic-like symptoms can occur with all the anxiety disorders and there is a fair amount of co-occurrence among the anxiety disorders.' So if you have one anxiety disorder (your primary diagnosis), there's a good chance that you might have some characteristics of other disorders as well. No rest for the weary, eh?

OBSESSIVE-COMPULSIVE DISORDER

You probably noticed that the term 'obsessive-compulsive' is hyphenated. That's because this particular disorder has two parts – the obsessive part and the compulsive part, or the 'O' and the 'C'. Let's start with the 'O', which most often takes the form of obsessive or recurring intrusive thoughts. These thoughts can include a haunting image or the repetition of unpleasant words or phrases. It's like when you get a really bad song stuck in your head and it plays over and over again – basically the same thing, only a lot worse.

Here's a list of a few common obsessions:

- ordering, where one feels compelled to place an item in a designated spot or order
- perfectionism, which means constantly checking for one's own mistake or error
- fear of contamination, for example, through a handshake or by touching an object
- superstition, especially associated with numbers, most notably positive numbers and the numbers seven and 13 [22]

But doesn't everyone have an occasional unpleasant thought, or prefer things in their proper place, or jam useless junk into their attic? Who among us would walk under a ladder, chase a black cat, or crack a mirror if we didn't have to? What makes an OCDer different? According to the experts, if the obsession or compulsion causes marked anxiety and is time-consuming, meaning it takes up more than one hour per day, that could warrant the diagnosis of OCD.[23]

Now let's talk about the 'C', which stands for compulsively engaging in specific rituals of behaviour in order to reduce anxiety. While these rituals often differ from person to person, the behaviour model is the same: an obsessive thought gives rise to anxiety, and this anxiety is then reduced or relieved by compulsive behaviours.[24] So let's say you have some obsessive thinking, and this thinking gives rise to anxiety. The only way to relieve your anxiety is to perform a compulsive or ritualistic behaviour – you wash your hands or twist the lock on the door, once or twice or three times. But what happens when you stop? You guessed it, the anxiety returns.

Now let's see what our old friend the DSM has to say about OCD.

Obsessive-Compulsive Disorder is characterized by obsessions (which cause marked anxiety or distress) and/or by compulsions (which serve to neutralize anxiety).

A lot of big, scary words there: obsession, compulsion, distress ... What do they all mean? Let's start with the scariest one.

Obsession. Hey, wait a minute! Isn't that the name of that pricey perfume found at posh department stores? If it's so bad, why are people paying top money and spritzing it all over themselves? And what exactly is an obsession, anyway?

Obsess: to haunt or trouble in mind; to beset; to harass.

(There it is again, that whole trouble in the mind thing.)

Obsession: the fact or state of being obsessed with an idea, desire, or emotion.

(Well, that certainly doesn't sound like any fun.)

Compulsion: an irresistible impulse to perform some irrational act.

(Like typing the last word of each sentence three times. Times. Times. Times.)

What exactly does it mean to obsess? Well, a hundred years ago you would have been diagnosed with the 'doubting sickness', which is still a fairly good description of the disorder today.

Let's say a classic OCDer – we'll call him Stanley – wants to take his dog, Nashville, to the park. So he clips on Nashville's lead and steps out of his kitchen door, making sure to lock it. We mean *absolutely* sure to lock it; you know, turning the lock back and forth to hear that comforting 'click' again and again. Stanley would like to hear that click a couple more times, but Nashville's tugging at the lead because he really loves the park.

Finally, they head down the street and Nashville's tail is wagging, but Stanley hears this little voice in the back of his mind whispering, 'What if the kitchen door isn't locked?' It's hard for Stanley to ignore the voice – in fact, it's already causing him some anxiety – but Nashville can see the park now and he's practically dragging Stanley down the street. Suddenly the tiny voice is not so tiny. Now the voice is shouting, and with each shout the anxiety escalates, and in no time at all it blossoms into a full-blown panic attack. So Stanley turns round and rushes home, dragging a disappointed Nashville behind him. He gets to the kitchen door and checks the lock, turning it back and forth to hear that comforting click, and slowly the anxiety subsides.

The voice plants the seed of doubt that overrides all logic. Hence, the doubting sickness.

Panic diary

Julie at age 44

2 December 2002

Dear Diary,

It happens every day. Sometimes it happens first thing in the morning, before my eyes are open, when just the mind is awake. Sometimes it happens only when I move, like when I get out of bed and start walking to the kitchen. It's like I can't engage in any repetitive motion without counting it out.

It's not like I *have* to count the steps to get to the kitchen. It's just this voice. This incessant voice and all she does is count the motions. One, two, three, four, one, two, three, four. Sometimes it goes up to eight, sometimes to 16, then 32, then 64. When it's happening this way, when I'm counting by the square roots of 'two' or 'three' I know something's wrong. I know I'm afraid of something, but I don't even know what it is because when I'm counting this way, it's like someone else has begun the counting and I only hear it after it's already begun.

So there I am, in a shop or in the kitchen or in the car or walking upstairs and there's the voice, the number voice. Counting away.

I can tell what kind of shape I'm in by the way the voice counts. If it's counting *real fast*, I know I'm in a little bit of trouble. If I'm aware of the counting from the start, like I usually am when I count along with the motions of my body, when I walk, walk, walk, one, two, three, then it's just sort of irritating. I want to say, 'Just shut up.' It's like I live right next door to someone who just won't shut up. But I know that someone is me, so I try to be nice to her, try not to tell her to shut up, although, really, sometimes I wish she just would. The counting happens when I'm alone and when I'm not alone. It happens when I'm at home and when I'm not at home. It happens across the table in a restaurant or when I leave the table to go to the ladies. And it's not just me that I count for. Sometimes I count for others, count the steps the waiter takes as I'm aware of him approaching and leaving the table. Nothing fancy. Nothing elaborate, just one, two, three, four. Or in the car, when the indicator clicks on, I can't hear it without counting it and even after it clicks off, I'm still counting the repetitive motion of the sound.

If I suddenly become aware of the counting, I know I'm in more than a little bit of trouble. Or if the counting is really fast, then I know something big time is going on. But the worst is when I'm way up in the high numbers, when I suddenly find myself at 128,000 then 256,000 then 512,000 then 1,024,000. I know I'm in trouble then because I don't remember when it started, I don't remember starting at two, then going to four, then eight, then 16. But I know something made me start, and I know that whatever that something was, it's something that made me afraid. Afraid enough to shut down for a split second. I think that's when the counter wakes up, I think she starts counting right after I've been afraid. I think she counts to fill the tiny spaces of each moment that were wiped clean, wiped clean as in eradicated, by fear. I think she counts until the moments start to flow back together again.

Indulging the compulsion – counting, washing, locking and unlocking – relieves the anxiety and fear. The thought, 'Is the kitchen door really locked?' is the obsessive thought. Checking the door, again and again, is the ritual that relieves the anxiety. A great example is Jack Nicholson's character in the hit film, *As Good As It Gets*. He touches a doorknob and that little voice pipes up, 'That doorknob is probably covered with thousands of microscopic germs.' This causes his anxiety to kick in, so he rushes to the bathroom and scrubs his hands with hot soapy water. Then there's that voice again, 'Are you sure you got all the germs?' followed by more hand washing, and so it goes on.

There are no rules on the 'how' of obsessive thoughts. Sometimes they'll strike suddenly, ploughing into you without warning, and other times they'll sneak up gradually, building slowly over a period of time. For some OCDers, the experience is exactly the same each time. For others, it's a whole different ball game each time out. It's a completely individual matter.

UNDRESSING IN PUBLIC AND OTHER FUN STUFF YOU'LL NEVER DO

Sometimes the obsession has nothing to do with a compulsion; sometimes the obsession comes in the form of an impulse. Unfortunately, often it's an impulse to do harm to someone you love, quite frequently your child, which is a particularly horrifying thought. However, it's such a common impulse that it is listed in a paragraph of specific obsessions in the DSM:[25] 'Aggressive or horrific impulses, e.g. to hurt one's child or to shout an obscenity in church', and sexual imagery (e.g. a recurrent pornographic image).

It's important to understand that an obsessive thought is just what it sounds like – it's a thought that you obsess about. It's not a wish to actually hurt someone. In her pioneering book *Hope and Help for Your Nerves*, Dr Claire Weekes tells the story of a paediatric nurse who passed in front of an open window one day while holding an infant in her arms. As she passed the window she had a thought: 'Wouldn't it be awful if I threw this baby out of the window?'[26] It was a fleeting thought. A non-OCDer might barely notice it, or if she did, she'd probably forget it.

This nurse, in her stressful state, was horrified by it and that very horror gave the thought power. It became an obsessive thought, and the harder the nurse tried to push the thought away, the more firmly embedded it became. She had to pass the window holding a child many times each day. The thought tormented her. According to Dr Weekes, the woman had no real wish to harm the child, and as a matter of fact this was the last thing the nurse would ever do. Her wish was to simply be rid of the obsessive thought.

So, what's the best way to be rid of an obsessive thought?

Stop trying.

That's right, stop trying to push the thought away. By accepting the thought as just that – a thought – over time, the thought will slowly begin to lose its power. The thought won't magically disappear, but eventually it will begin to fade and it will no longer cause you anguish, because it truly is only a thought.

Many who struggle with this form of OCD – where the obsessive thought is an impulse – don't receive the proper diagnosis or get help because they simply cannot bring themselves to speak out loud the impulsive thoughts that plague them. Sometimes known as the 'Pure-O',[27] this arm of OCD is like a different room in the house of panic. It's not the supermarket you have to run out of, it's not Perry's car or the restaurant that fuels your anxiety and starts the whole fight or flight mechanism – it's a thought, a horrific thought that you can neither quiet nor evict.

Now impulses can be a real drag, that's for sure, but they should not be confused with the delusional thoughts and bizarre behaviours that occur in schizophrenia.[28] Don't skip this part, because it's important. Unlike the schizophrenic, the OCDer realizes that these thoughts are coming from his own mind; he doesn't believe that he is being sent messages from someone or somewhere else. Also, the OCDer is 'ego-dystonic', meaning that he finds the obsessive thought repugnant and is genuinely appalled by it.

Panic diary
Tony at age 50
6 June 2003

Dear Diary,
So much of my discomfort was due to my fear of going insane. This was in the late 1970s, and you have to remember, none of this was talked about back then. It was a very tough time for me. I was plagued by feelings of being different. It was an intense and uncomfortable feeling, being different from everyone else. I felt that I was sick and that no one would understand my sickness.

That was also the time in my life when I had just graduated from college and my brothers and sisters were having babies. We'd all be at my parents' house and everyone would lay the babies on the living room floor. I would be sitting on the couch. And then everyone would leave the room. I was terrified. One of my biggest fears was that I would just get up and ... trample them – that I would kill my own nephews. No one ever knew. It was horrible to sit on that couch and have those thoughts.

But my problem wasn't on any list back in the 1970s. I was afraid to even talk to my shrink about it. I just remember those years as being so painful. But finally I did talk about it. That really helped me. I discovered that the very fact that I was agonizing over having such thoughts suggested that I wouldn't do it. I learnt that people who really do these types of things have no conscience. They don't think about it or worry about it. The fact that you are driving yourself nuts about these thoughts means that you have a strong sense of conscience.

There were other things, too. I went to a lot of concerts back then. I would listen while a pianist played beautiful music and I would have thoughts of taking my gum out of my mouth and flinging it at the pianist. Or sometimes it would happen at church, right at the moment of the consecration, a very solemn moment, and I would be afraid that I was going to start shouting obscenities. I shared this with a close friend once and he said he had the exact same thought in church, but that the thought made him chuckle, rather than scared him.

Sometimes people would unwittingly say things that would stay with me and haunt me for years. Then, in 1993, my doctor prescribed Prozac. I can't even begin to tell you how my quality of life changed after that. It's remarkable a pill could do that; I mean, it's a miracle.

Like many other anxiety disorders, OCD tends to run on a continuum, ranging from mild and relatively manageable to complex and not at all manageable. Also like other anxiety disorders, there really is no definitive answer to the question, 'What causes OCD?' However, there are theories.

We'll start with what we'll call the Pet Theory. Not pet as in dog or cat or iguana, but PET as in positron emission tomography, which is a technique used to study the brain. PET studies compared the brain activity of people with OCD to people with other mental illnesses and people with no mental illness (bet that line was short!). The findings were definite: the brain of the OCDers appeared different from the other brains.[29] The results of this study suggest that OCD has a neurobiological basis.

Not too long ago, back when theories weren't nearly as good as they are today, OCD was often thought to stem from 'family problems or to attitudes learned in childhood – for example, an inordinate emphasis on cleanliness, or a belief that certain thoughts are dangerous or unacceptable'. Glad those days are over!

Another theory, one we like to call the Gate Theory, also operates on the assumption that the OCD brain is different, but that the cause of this difference is probably attributable to physical or mental trauma to the brain, or possibly through heredity. According to this theory, within the brain there is a structure like a screen or a gate that acts to filter out thoughts, and when the brain is working correctly this structure screens out many irrelevant thoughts. However, a brain that is not working correctly may fail to screen out these thoughts – it may fail to close the 'gate' that sends these thoughts to the conscious reasoning part of the brain.[30] That'll teach you to see if you closed the door behind you, won't it?

Then there's the Catastrophic Thinking Theory. Dr Paul Salkovskis of Oxford University believes that the OCD brain started out like any other brain, but that through years of catastrophic thinking, usually due to one's upbringing, eventually one develops a fear of the catastrophic thoughts. Soon the OCDer begins to believe the thoughts are dangerous and eventually the thoughts become obsessive.

Theories! Theories! Theories! How about some cold, hard facts? For instance, did you know that 2.3 per cent of the US population (3.3 million Americans) experiences OCD in a given year? How about this one: 3.7 per cent of the US population (approximately 5.3 million Americans) suffers from social phobia in a given year.[31] You're probably wondering what social phobia is. We're glad you asked.

SOCIAL PHOBIA *OR* TO FLEE OR NOT TO FLEE? THAT IS THE QUESTION

Remember Snow White's sidekick, Bashful? Never got more than a blush and a stutter out of him, did she? Was Bashful just shy, or could it have been something more? Is it possible that Bashful suffered from social phobia? Let's take a look at what the DSM has to say:

Social phobia is characterized by clinically significant anxiety provoked by exposure to certain types of social or performance situations, often leading to avoidance behaviour.[32]

This sounds like something we've all experienced. What's the difference between just being shy (or bashful) and social phobia? First of all, people with social phobia don't just blush and look at their feet, they experience a perpetual and chronic fear of embarrassment with symptoms as debilitating as:

- profuse sweating
- trembling
- flushing
- nausea
- urgency of micturition (urinating)
- panic attacks
- avoidance behaviour

Here's an example: Let's say you're at a fancy dinner party, or maybe a formal New Year's Eve bash (hey, it's our fantasy), and you notice that you've had a piece of toilet paper stuck to the bottom of your sexy black shoe the whole time you were out on the dance floor. How you react to this dilemma depends upon your individual personality. Perhaps you slyly tear off the offending tissue and continue to dance, basically employing an ignorance of the whole ordeal. Or perhaps, you spot the tissue, then call everyone's attention to it, and you all get a good laugh.

If you struggle with social phobia, you might rush from the dance floor, completely humiliated, and lock yourself inside the tiny lavatory cubicle for the rest of the night. Actually, if you struggle with social phobia, you probably wouldn't be on the dance floor. In fact, you probably wouldn't even be at the party.

But let's say you did go. Let's say you went with Perry and, while he's joking and laughing with his pals at the bar, you're on the dance floor where you spot the offending tissue. Maybe you feel the room get a little hazy. Maybe you feel a tightening in your chest. Maybe your heart starts to pound. You're having a panic attack.

You might think of social phobia as a specific phobia of social settings. While this may sound like just one thing, when you think about it, it's rather profound and far-reaching. It's true that social phobia doesn't get a lot of press, so there can be the temptation to underestimate the toll that this disorder takes on the lives of those who find themselves in its grip.

Panic diary
Shannon at age 15
11 January 2004

Dear Diary,
I am 15 and I go to a high school with a large number of students – about 2,500. There are sometimes 36 students in a classroom, so you can imagine how very stressful it is for a socially defunct person like me.

I started getting panic attacks a few months ago. The day the first one happened, I had about two hours of sleep the night before and in the morning I drank some coffee. I was in my World History class, which is the most stressful of all the classes I have.

The whole morning I had felt kind of out of it and really tired. I was sitting in my seat trying not to fall asleep, when suddenly my heart started beating really quickly. And then I couldn't breathe. I had no idea what was going on and I was scared out of my mind. I remember thinking it was hell.

So I raised my hand and asked if I could go to the nurse. Before I got to the office, I went to the toilet and cried because I thought there was something wrong with me. What, I didn't know. I thought I would die.

> My dad picked me up from school and took me home. My parents passed off my first panic attack as a caffeine thing. Then, a month later, I drank coffee again and freaked out so badly I was screaming to be taken to the hospital.
>
> That was when I swore off caffeine. I thought my panic attacks were caused by it, but I was wrong. Lately, I have been having them nearly every day. The days I don't have them, it's been really close.
>
> Today I had another panic attack – a bad one. I have been ill for a couple days and I was dizzy. I started thinking there was something wrong with me. Why had I been tired the whole day? Why was I dizzy? Why couldn't I think clearly? So I started crying. I thought I had some serious disease or I was crazy. My dad read to me and it went away after a couple of minutes. That has been my experience.

Social phobias typically begin in adolescence in smaller social settings. The fear of scrutiny by others or the anguish of embarrassing oneself often leads to the avoidance of social situations altogether.

The fear itself might be specific, such as eating or drinking in public, speaking in public, or any encounter with the opposite sex. It might include a fear of vomiting in public or any specific behaviour that would result in feelings of humiliation. For some, direct eye-to-eye contact is unbearable. Or the fear may be non-specific, arising from virtually any social situation outside of the immediate family.[33] Bashful would be okay with Sleepy and Sneezy and Dopey and Happy and the rest of them, but things might get tough when he had to turn up for jury service. You get the point.

People with social phobia realize that their fear is unreasonable. This awareness is part of the criteria for the disorder. They'll experience great anticipatory anxiety prior to social engagements, and over time the disorder will likely cause a disruption in their normal routine, such as an inability to attend school, or go to work, or even have any social activities or relationships whatsoever.

Although the 'why' of social phobia is unknown, one study implicates a glitch in the small structure inside the brain that we discussed earlier, the amygdala, which controls our fear responses. Other research, through animal studies, suggests that social phobia may be the work of a gene and therefore hereditary. Still another theory implicates a biochemical basis for the disorder ... and then there are the environmental influences ... Are you seeing a pattern here?

DANCING WITH PANIC: THE TANGO

The idea of the panic tango is to pull your panic close. We know this might sound just plain loony, but hear us out. By now you understand that the physical symptoms you experience during a panic attack are simply due to the adrenalin pumping through your body, and are triggered by the flight or fight response. By changing that response you can stop the adrenalin, which in turn will stop your symptoms.

During a panic attack

Start with the panic waltz, then foxtrot and face your panic. Now tango, go cheek to cheek with your panic. The panic tango is about absolutely accepting your panic. Since we are biologically predisposed to running from fear, you have to override that initial impulse and instead turn towards the panic. Grab it by the waist and pull it close. You have to fully commit to this concept for it to succeed. If at first it doesn't work, keep trying.

In the beginning you may experience only small moments of relief during your panic attack, but with continued practice this dance step can actually stop a panic attack in its tracks. The trick is not to run from panic, but to dance with it. As Claire Weekes has written, 'Recovery lies on the other side of panic. Recovery lies in the places you fear.'

ADDITIONAL FUN FACTS TO IMPRESS YOUR FRIENDS

- Social phobia occurs twice as often in women as in men, although a higher percentage of men seek help for this particular disorder
- OCD was once thought to be caused by early experiences related to one's toilet training (we're not kidding)

4 POST-TRAUMATIC STRESS DISORDER *OR* YOU CAN (AND OFTEN DO) TAKE IT WITH YOU

There is a core of anger in the soul of almost every veteran. In one man, it becomes a consuming flame that sears his soul and burns his body. In another it is barely traceable.[34]

WILLARD WALLER

POST-TRAUMATIC STRESS DISORDER is the big granddaddy of a class of anxiety disorders that develop as a result of exposure to trauma. The study of stress disorders, or 'psychotraumatology', as it's sometimes called, is a relatively new branch of psychiatry, only about 15 years old. Medical interest in trauma, on the other hand, is much older than that. It can be found as early as about 4,000 years ago, in the writings of the ancient Egyptians.[35]

The 'stress' in PTSD is not your everyday variety of stress. It's not the stress of juggling career and kids, or managing finances, or caring for ageing parents; it's a very specific notion of stress. It's the physiological and psychological stress that arises as the direct result of exposure to a traumatic event.

But people are exposed to traumas all the time. Well, maybe not all the time, but many people are exposed to trauma and not all of them develop PTSD. Just like many people are exposed to rhinoviruses, but not all of them come down with colds. There are billions of germs that we're all exposed to every day, but most of us manage to stay fairly healthy. Why is that?

The same question can be asked of our response to trauma. Some people who experience trauma go on to live happier, healthier lives. Somehow the trauma serves to bring sharply into focus what's most important in life. Other people do not respond in a positive or 'adaptive' way to trauma. For these people, trauma can literally stop their life in its tracks and send them spiralling into a self-contained prison, a prison in which they feel trapped in an endless repetition of some aspect of the trauma.

If panic attacks are the sneezes of anxiety disorders, then PTSD is a disorder in the immune system. Something's gone awry, something in the mind or brain or spirit of the person, that prevents them from processing the trauma or that prevents them from 'getting over it' the way someone can get over a fever.

This brings us to one of the more perplexing features of PTSD – its longevity, or what is sometimes referred to as a 'lack of extinction'. This means that the illness keeps on going long after the cause of the illness has ceased to exist. It's a mysterious thing, this PTSD; so baffling, in fact, that at present some experts suggest we may be only at the tip of the iceberg. Listen to this: 'a thoughtful examination will show that the complexity of the phenomena of PTSD will raise more questions than science can provide answers to at the present time.'[36]

A LONG TIME COMING ... THE HISTORY OF PTSD

PTSD was originally conceived as a disorder experienced by Vietnam veterans and was initially called 'Post-Vietnam Syndrome'. Today, the disorder is broadly applied to a wide variety of traumas and is recognized as a serious public health problem affecting as many as 25 million Americans at some point in their lives.[37]

Even though PTSD wasn't an 'official' disorder until 1980, the idea that soldiers are exposed to trauma during war is not a new idea. There are medical references to a condition known as 'soldier's heart' that date back to the American Civil War. Freud introduced the notion of 'war neurosis' (seems like he had something to say about everything) and, by the time WWII rolled around, phrases like 'combat fatigue' and 'shell shock' were commonly used to describe the effects of war on combatants.

Even though these phrases were in use, many veterans must have suffered in silence with the symptoms now associated with PTSD. Symptoms such as *persistent nightmares* of swimming through the bloody waters of Normandy Beach. The war's been over for ten years, but not for you. It's still raging every night in your dreams. Symptoms such as *sudden outbursts of anger* or occasional *lapses in memory*. It's Sunday morning and your wife's frying eggs, but all you can smell is the scent of gunpowder, so you grab the frying pan and fling it against the wall. Again. Only you don't know it's 'again' because you don't remember the other times that you did it. You also don't know why you *startle so easily*, or why you're *afraid of crowds*, or why certain high-pitched sounds make you glance at the sky, waiting for the B-52s to empty their bellies.

War is hell. War has always been hell. But when Vietnam veterans returned home, it wasn't to flag waving, grateful crowds; it was to an anti-war movement that had divided America. The vets were not, to put it mildly, given a hero's welcome.[38] But they were suffering. Suffering from the mysterious symptoms of a disease that in 1970 did not yet have a name.

Like the other anxiety disorders we've discussed, PTSD did not officially exist until its inclusion in the 1980 DSM and it is probably the only entry in the entire DSM that was put there as a result of personal advocacy by those who suffered its symptoms – the Vietnam veterans. The vets just started talking to each other and found that they were all experiencing the same kind of symptoms. So they kept talking. Then they brought in psychiatrists to listen. Soon there were thousands of them and it was largely due to their efforts that PTSD made it into the DSM.

A pioneering study showed a staggering incidence of PTSD in Vietnam vets: it estimated that '30 percent of the 3.1 million Vietnam veterans who saw active duty developed PTSD sometime after the war.'[39]

In the twenty or so years since its inclusion in the DSM, much has been learned about PTSD. This disorder now applies to victims of a wide variety of traumas, from war to 'hostage taking, rape, family abuse, natural disasters, accidents, death of a loved one',[40] and most recently, to terrorist acts. Programmes, health centres and organizations devoted to the study of PTSD exist in America, Australia, Canada, Europe, Israel and elsewhere.[41]

REMEMBRANCES OF THINGS PAST

Stated in simple terms, PTSD is a condition that arises following exposure to a traumatic event. The DSM offers a lengthy and highly specific description. We'll break it into parts. The first part covers direct experience:

PTSD is the development of characteristic symptoms following exposure to an extreme traumatic stressor involving direct personal experience of an event that involves actual or threatened death or serious injury or other threat to one's physical integrity.[42]

Some of the 'traumatic stressors' associated with the development of PTSD include:

- combat
- violent personal assault
- being kidnapped
- being taken hostage
- terrorist attack
- torture
- incarceration as a prisoner of war or in a concentration camp
- natural or man-made disasters
- severe car accidents
- being diagnosed with a life-threatening illness

The second part of the definition involves *indirect experience* of the above kinds of traumas: 'witnessing an event that involves death, injury, or a threat to the physical integrity of another person; or learning about unexpected or violent death, serious harm, or threat of death or injury experienced by a family member or other close associate.'[43]

In addition to directly or indirectly experiencing one (or more) of the above sorts of traumas, a person's response to the event must involve:

- intense fear
- helplessness
- horror

PTSD develops as the result of a direct or indirect experience with a traumatic event that elicits feelings of intense fear, helplessness, or horror – like having a gun held to your head or seeing the World Trade Center crumble to the ground on 11 September 2001.

Panic diary
Faith at age 33
24 December 2001

Dear Diary,
I've lived through history. I've seen the end of the Cold War, the fall of the Berlin Wall, the rebirth of the eastern European nations of my heritage. I've witnessed the birth of the Internet and the beginning of the information age. I've watched nations rise and fall, people rise and fall, the world evolve into a band of people united electronically in a community of strength.
  I've lived through history. But nothing prepared me.
  I saw the World Trade Center fall.
  I cannot comprehend it. I've watched the trucks carting rubble out of the site. I've been past military and police checkpoints. I've watched the smoke rise high into the sky. I've seen my city become a war zone. I've been to a memorial service. I've cried rivers of tears.
  The images come to me when I least expect them. I'll be walking down the street and it all comes back, my brain

> replaying the day like some warped VCR. I try to fight it back, but it comes anyway.
>
> I fight against it, but at the same time do not want to forget even the smallest detail. I don't want to lose even the smallest bit of anger or terror or grief. I want to carry the images with me for ever.
>
> And I will. A piece of me will always be buried in the rubble, trapped in the smoke, and for ever looking upward into the southern sky for that which is no longer there. 2001 is leaving us quickly now. It is taking a part of me with it.

'Taking a part of me with it' – that's how victims of trauma often refer to themselves: without a single, whole sense of self. Instead they feel like a self made of pieces, like the pieces of rubble in a war-torn city.

A SIMPLE TWIST OF FATE

There's a cruel irony at work in PTSD. In the other anxiety disorders, a panic attack is a misfiring of the fight or flight mechanism, but PTSD begins with exposure to a trauma. In other words, it begins when you're face to face with a real external threat. Someone is pointing a gun at your head. Hurricane Andrew just tore the roof off your primary school. You just dropped your child off at the Murrah Federal building in downtown Oklahoma City and it's 19 April 1995.

In response to the trauma, your fight or flight mechanism fires up. Your body is pumping into your bloodstream everything necessary for the fight or flight of your life. As long as the terror continues, as long as the external event continues to unfold, your body will keep you ready to fight or flee. However, when the threat passes and the danger is gone, it's as if the fight or flight response is stuck in the 'on' position. While this may be great for fighting or flying, it's really lousy for sleeping, processing memories, sustaining positive, loving relationships, or being fully engaged in the here and now.

Although the event of the trauma begins to fade, aspects of your experience at the time of trauma are carried forward into the present and continue to affect you as if they're occurring right at the present moment.

Let's say you're on a white beach, enjoying a stunning pink sunset while sipping Bahama Mamas with that certain someone. Sounds good? Now imagine if this experience could be preserved in all its reality, in all its crystalline clarity, by magically transforming it into a golden dust – a special golden dust that you can keep in a phial, to open whenever you want and sprinkle over yourself. And whenever you do, there you are, back on that shimmering beach with that certain someone, with every feeling exactly the same.

That's what happens in PTSD, only it's not a shimmering beach – not even close. And you have no control over when that little phial is opened or when that dust is sprinkled over you. It comes with no warning or desire. It could be a day or a week or month or even a year later, before you develop symptoms.

If you're in a high-risk population, as are veterans and policemen and rescue workers, you're more likely to develop symptoms. Homeless mothers have a 36 per cent rate of PTSD (three times the normal rate for women in the general population).[44] Children exposed to domestic violence have a staggering 95 per cent incidence rate of PTSD.[45]

To receive a diagnosis of PTSD, you must experience at least one symptom from each of the three categories listed in the DSM:

1. Persistent re-experience of the traumatic event
- recurrent and intrusive distressing recollections of the event
- recurrent distressing dreams of the event
- feeling as if the traumatic event were recurring

2. Persistent avoidance of stimuli associated with the traumatic event
- persistent efforts to avoid thoughts, feelings, conversations, activities, places or people that arouse recollections of the trauma

3. Persistent symptoms of increased arousal or alertness
- irritability or outbursts of anger
- hypervigilance
- exaggerated startle response

There are other symptoms associated with PTSD as well. The following is a partial list:

- illusions
- hallucinations
- disassociative flashback episodes
- inability to recall an important aspect of the trauma
- feeling of detachment or estrangement from others
- sense of foreshortened future
- difficulty falling or staying asleep

Notice that some of these symptoms overlap with symptoms of panic attacks. That's because PTSD has a high co-occurrence among the anxiety disorders. This means that if you have PTSD, you have an 80 per cent chance of having a related disorder, such as panic attacks, depression or alcoholism.[46]

With PTSD, panic attacks can be brought on by almost anything associated with the original trauma. These associations are called triggers, and triggers come in two varieties: external triggers and internal triggers. External triggers include things like smells or sights or sounds, but they can be less obvious than that; even the reminder of the forthcoming anniversary of an event can cause an attack.

Panic diary
Rachel at age 51
2 November 2003

Dear Diary,
It's a few weeks before Thanksgiving, and the shops are filled with everything Christmas. I'm starting to see the images again. You know the ones I'm talking about, the ones I tell you about every year at this time. In case you've forgotten, I'll tell you again.

It was New Year's Eve and I was ten years old. I was alone in my bedroom, having a party all by myself. It was getting close to midnight and I was watching Guy Lombardo and the million or so people gathered in Times Square in New York City, all of them glancing up at the crystal ball that would fall at the stroke of midnight.

I'd been turning up the volume of the television louder and louder throughout the night, trying to drown out the sounds of my father's voice and the sounds of what he might be doing to my mother. I'd heard some already. The thud of her body against the plaster wall, then all quiet on the Western Front until the next big roar.

Even though the television was loud, I was starting to hear some of those sounds. I tried to focus on the TV, on all those people ringing out the old year and bringing in the new one. They started counting: ten, nine, eight … That's when I heard her. Seven, six, five … And I heard her again, not clearly, but she was yelling, yelling something. Three, two, one …

The ball drops. The people are singing that stupid song, but all I can hear is her screaming, screaming words I muffle out but then I hear them, somehow they break through, and what they say is this: 'You're killing me, you're killing me.' Then a scream and I'm running to the back bedroom, to his bedroom, and I hear a smack, a smack, crack, smacking sound of I don't know what. Then I'm there. She's on the bed and he's leaning over her, a fat brass candlestick in his hand …

You know the rest, how I ran out of the house, ran as fast as I could with one purpose and one purpose only: to scream into the cold dark sky, to scream out to the windows of neighbours, something, anything, so that he wouldn't kill her. But when I got to the porch and opened my mouth, nothing at all came out. Not a squeak. Not a peep. Not even a breath. Where had the scream gone, I wondered? Was it still inside me somewhere or had I run into a wall, a wall of glass that took away my voice?

How long ago is that now? 41 years and here I am, a woman in the middle of life, but each year at this time, it's like I'm a haunted house. The very thought of Thanksgiving makes my heart start to pound, because then it's only six more weeks until that moment when the world welcomes in another year.

An external trigger – a Christmas carol playing over the loudspeaker of a shop – is all it takes to open that little phial. But internal triggers, like a word, a thought, or an idea, can open the phial, too. It doesn't have to be uppermost in your mind. Even dreams can make your heart start hammering as you relive the trauma again and again.

Panic diary
Faith at age 34
17 March 2002

Dear Diary,
Horrible nightmare last night. I was at work, but some of us were sitting on the grassy bank of a river or in some grassy field that had a perfect view of Manhattan. There were work people, but not really work people. We ate lunch and watched missiles flying in all directions. I remember thinking one was headed in Patti's direction and trying to call her. Then a plane dive-bombed the Brooklyn Bridge, really the area we thought was the Brooklyn Bridge, because we couldn't tell.

We were all very unfazed by this, and decided to go back up to the office for a better view. I was very anxious; I kept trying to find people to leave with me but everyone just told me I was overreacting and to calm down.

Someone was sitting in an office saying, 'No biggie', over and over again. It's even more blurry after this ... I get trapped or stuck in the lift, and it takes a while to get to the ground. There's chaos in the streets but I'm very detached from it.

Then it isn't really chaos, and buildings are falling, planes are crashing into everything, but no one is worried except me.

A THEORETICAL TOUR

Freud had some good theories about war neurosis, which could very well apply to PTSD. He suggested that 'war trauma creates a breach in a hypothetical stimulus barrier that normally protects the mental apparatus from excessive amounts of excitation.'[47] This means that the traumatic event is simply more than the human mind (or at least some human minds) can tolerate. Freud suggests that the 'mental apparatus' (we're pretty sure he means 'the mind' here) is subjected to a hypothetical 'repetition compulsion'.[48] In essence, the mind is replaying the event or pieces of the event over and over again. As the authors of *Post-Traumatic Stress Disorder* state, 'the repetitive phenomena in traumatic neurosis do not necessarily constitute progress toward self-healing; they often express traumatic surrender of the psychic apparatus to a new set of rules.'[49]

Another theory centres on the notion that PTSD alters the information processing systems of the brain. The brain processes and stores information and, while doing so, it tosses a lot of stuff into the trash. It's not clear why some things stay and others go, but the general idea is that the PTSD brain is no longer able to function in this normal way. Maybe the brain is clogged with all the unprocessed information from the original traumatic event and so, basically, it just keeps trying. Hence, the eternal return of persistent thoughts and images.

There is a Japanese word, *hibakusha*, that translates roughly as 'frozen dream'. This word was coined to describe the dreamlike state of mind of survivors of the bombings at Hiroshima and Nagasaki. As those who suffer from PTSD know all too well, when it comes to trauma, the past literally is the present. You can, and often do, take it with you.

But you don't have to take it all with you. There are treatments, medications and cutting-edge therapies that have shown great promise. We'll take a look at these in the following chapters.

DANCING WITH PANIC: THE TWIST

This isn't really a technique, it's more of a 'twist' on a technique. This was a heavy chapter, so the puzzle is meant to help you relax. Did you know that solving a puzzle can reduce muscle tension? Okay, we just made that up, but it probably won't increase muscle tension. So, grab a pencil and get comfortable. We've hidden ten words in the puzzle. Each of these ten words appeared in the chapter you've just read. When you're done you can check your answers on page 147 ... now what did we do with those answers?

F	X	G	O	L	D	D	U	S	T
L	O	I	L	E	U	P	P	T	A
A	P	V	I	E	T	N	A	M	L
S	H	R	V	R	R	H	N	O	M
H	R	U	A	O	A	I	G	O	Q
B	N	S	A	C	U	J	E	L	U
A	H	F	D	S	M	V	R	A	D
C	R	N	S	T	A	R	T	L	E
K	I	O	A	R	L	U	K	T	E
M	U	G	P	A	N	I	C	I	M

5 A BAD MOOD RISIN'

I felt like I was on death row.[50]

TERRY BRADSHAW, PRO FOOTBALL COMMENTATOR
AND HALL OF FAME QUARTERBACK

MOOD DISORDERS ARE EXACTLY what they sound like: disorders of your mood, which should not be confused with 'having a bad day'.

Everyone experiences lousy moods sometimes. Maybe your good friend Perry is moving away or maybe you didn't get that promotion at the office after you put in all of that overtime. But feeling sad or feeling depressed is not the same as the medical disorder known as depression. You may be wondering what depression is doing in a book about panic. Does depression cause panic attacks? Well, no. But there is a link between anxiety and depression. Often panic attacks that occur out of the blue occur during depression. [51]

This doesn't mean that everyone with depression will also experience panic attacks. It also doesn't mean that everyone who has panic attacks is depressed. However, depression is associated with a high frequency of anxiety symptoms and anxiety disorders. Our expert, Dr Charles, says that about three-quarters of the time he sees depression occur with anxiety.

But what exactly is depression? What's the difference between simply feeling low and a major depressive episode? To be diagnosed with depression, you must experience at least five of the following symptoms for at least a two-week period, representing a change from your previous functioning:[52]

Criteria for Major Depressive Episode
- depressed mood
- diminished interest or pleasure in activities
- significant appetite or weight loss or gain
- insomnia or hypersomnia
- feelings of worthlessness or excessive guilt
- diminished ability to think or concentrate
- recurrent thoughts of death or suicide

There can be other signs as well, such as a drastic drop in self-confidence, a general loss of vitality, a diminished sex drive, extremely slow speech, and delusions or hallucinations.

Depression isn't a new disease. Descriptions of it can be found in the writings of the Greek philosopher Hippocrates (460–370 BC). Back then it was referred to as melancholia, which translates, unfortunately, as 'black bile'.

Interestingly enough, melancholia was treated as a disease even then, meaning doctors believed that the depressed person was ill and so their bodily constitution was treated ... right up to the Middle Ages, anyway. About that time, religion took over and anyone struggling with a psychiatric disorder of any kind was considered either a sinner or possessed by a demon. As you might guess, the treatment options for possession and sinners left a little to be desired.

By the nineteenth century things were looking up. Typically someone suffering from depression during that period was sent to the countryside or to distant family members for some 'special care'. Sounds sort of like a holiday, doesn't it? When Abraham Lincoln was a young man, on more than one occasion he was sent to 'holiday' with his relatives in Kentucky.

In the twentieth century, Sigmund Freud chimed in, claiming that depression was rooted in an unconscious conflict, resulting in anger turned inwards. Of course, Freud believed depression could be cured through the process of psychoanalysis. His results weren't great, and psychoanalysis is no longer the treatment of choice for depression. With the introduction of antidepressants in the 1950s, the pendulum swung back and depression was again considered a medical condition – a disease – and treated accordingly.

Panic diary
Sean at age 50
1 December 2003

Dear Diary,
I had my first major depressive episode when I was finishing my senior year of college in the mid-1970s. I didn't have a clue as to what was going on, which was very frightening, I just felt disconnected from myself. I lost about 9 kilos. I couldn't eat. I had a thought about myself that was unreal, that was a fantasy, but it took hold as a reality. I remember sitting in a lecture hall one day, looking at a guy and thinking he was handsome, and then thinking, 'Oh my God, I'm gay.' And then

for days on end it was all I could think about. I obsessed upon thinking I was gay. That's what still happens today – I'll have a thought and it will stick to me for days on end. That's what anxiety is – it's a complete loss of perspective.

Growing up as an army brat, living in a lot of communities around the world had an effect on me. I didn't have a really strong sense of myself that you sometimes get from being rooted in a place. So any thought like that could more easily take hold, because I wasn't sure who I really was. That made the effect of this stuff stronger. It never occurred to me at the time that I was depressed. I just thought life had taken a very strange turn. I climbed out of this episode as symptoms abated after about a year and a half.

The second major episode occurred around the time my first child was born, about six years after college. The symptoms were familiar, and revolved around finding flaws in myself that suddenly became magnified, that were far out of proportion to their place in my life. The basic storyline spinning around in my head had to do with finding myself to be an unfit father. Things in my personal life that I thought were unsavoyry, I obsessed about. I lost my father when I was in my teens, so I think I had a certain image to uphold, and I thought I must be this perfect father. There were things about myself that troubled me or that I thought were bad. Things that might not have troubled me in the past suddenly became very important.

I did talk to my family doctor back then, and I told him I was having some symptoms. He was a pretty cool guy and this was a progressive family practice. But before he'd refer me to a therapist he told me to read a book called *If You See Buddha in the Road Kill Him*. He created this burden for me: I needed to read this book and then I needed to write about what my symptoms were. It was kind of an odd thing, creating this obstacle to getting the care I needed. Of course, I never did any of that, so I never got any help at that time.

I go through cycles of depression, cycles where it gets very raw and then it gets better. After a while I regain perspective, the freak-out recedes, and life goes on. Because I wasn't medicated and I didn't go through therapy, clearly there are underlying things that have not been dealt with.

'Underlying things'. Often one of these underlying things can be the trigger that sends someone predisposed to depression into a downward spiral. Since depression clusters in families, having a relative with depression increases your chances of being predisposed to the disorder. One of the biggest obstacles for people struggling with depression is that they often don't realize that something is physically or medically wrong with them. On the other hand, sometimes people believe they are in a major depressive episode, but they're wrong.

For instance, grief or bereavement can cause a person to display many of the same behaviours that are characteristic of depression. But bereavement is not depression. Bereavement is the process someone goes through after the loss of a cherished loved one. Although that process can be long and intense and filled with despair, it is not depression. However, someone predisposed to depression could spiral into a depression after the loss of a loved one.

Although the cause of depression is still unknown, the research is ongoing. Until recently the strongest theory was the chemical imbalance theory, which suggested a shortage of serotonin or norepinephrine in the brain. The newest model suggests that unhealthy nerve cell connections in the part of the brain that creates our emotions could be the problem. Furthermore, recent experiments with mice show that antidepressant medication stimulates the growth of new hippocampal nerve cells, which form new connections with the old nerve cells.[53] So if depression is due to stalled nerve cell growth or simply faulty connections, what we're really talking about is just a little repair work.

BIPOLAR DISORDER *OR* I LEFT MY CAR IN SAN FRANCISCO

Bipolar disorder is characterized by one or more manic episodes, usually accompanied by major depressive episodes. In other words, gigantic mood swings. Bipolar suggests polar opposites: high and low, happy and sad. The major depressive episodes are at one end of the bipolar spectrum, and manic episodes or mania are at the other end.

The essence of mania is a state of excitement with an inflated sense of self, but it's so much more than that. Manic behaviour or mania can be characterized by elation, hyperactivity, accelerated speaking and thinking, irritability and almost always a loss of good judgement. Manic patients have energy, *so* much energy! Some have described it as the feeling of racing in a speeding car that's just about to spin out of control.

With bipolar disorder you might one day experience a depression so severe that you can't climb out of bed and the following day you might hop on a plane to Paris or spend your entire life's savings on a Jaguar. Impaired judgement is a strong indicator of manic behaviour and normal inhibitions go out of the window. Despite these indications, diagnosing bipolar disorder can sometimes be tricky. As Dr Charles says, 'Rarely does anyone come in to the doctor during their manic phase;

they feel super and they're out conquering the world. It's only during the depressed phase that you can ask them if they have periods of time where they've made very poor judgements, like [taking] an impulsive trip to Vegas, or [whether they have] had grandiose ideas.'

The history of mania as a condition dates back to ancient times, but it was Emil Kraepelin, in the late nineteenth century, who 'put the disorder on the map as a modern disease'.[54] Unfortunately, he had no idea how to treat it. That wasn't discovered until 1949, with the introduction of lithium. Regular use of the drug lithium can stabilize the drastic mood swings associated with bipolar disorder.

Panic diary
Tendzin Choegyal, the youngest sibling of His Holiness the XIV Dalai Lama
November 1997

From the age of three I was recognized as Ngari Rinpoche, a reincarnation of a lama and, according to tradition, I was to be a celibate or a monk and to lead a monk's life. It was only when I was 25 that I realized I didn't have a vocation for it and I became a layperson.

I met my wife at Darjeeling, we married in 1972, and I began teaching English and Mathematics in a Tibetan children's school. After that I joined the Dalai Lama's office and worked as the Dalai Lama's private secretary. Then I went into the army. It was an army of Tibetan men and women and it was called the Special Frontier Force. We were trained as commandos; we learnt parachute jumping and were trained in all weapons. Then I came back to the Dalai Lama's office and served in the Security Department for a while and then I was transferred back to the private secretary's office of the Dalai Lama again.

I served there for ten years, until I was diagnosed with manic depression and had to leave the job. I did nothing for about three years. I was 35 years old, but when I think back I must have suffered from the illness much earlier. Maybe even as early as when I was seven or eight. But of course I didn't know. In the early stages, there was no feeling of anxiety, but there was overwhelming sadness that almost paralysed me. But later anxiety came. I had my first real bout of depression with panic attacks at age 31 or 32.

Generally speaking, in our part of the world, in India, a lot of these illnesses are misunderstood. The popular belief is that the illness is caused by possession or something. Sadly, in many underdeveloped countries, this view is prevalent. But actually it is a chemical imbalance.

I had never come across anybody else who talked about this illness openly. For people who suffer, I think it is important to seek help, and not to be afraid to say that I am ill. There are wonderful medicines out there. I think that is most important, that people seek help.

My family was very understanding. But when you are ill, I don't think people's understanding lives up to what you want them to understand. You know they're not up to it. And I think there will be difficulty always. I think it is very important for people to be sensitive and to sympathize.

The main thing is the treatment, then everything will be all right.

I think meditation definitely helps because if you do it right there is a type of order to the karmic state. One comes to understand the workings of cause and effect. The main purpose of meditation is to calm the mind of all despair and negativity by encouraging or practising, or cultivating a better understanding of reality. Yes, cultivating a way by which we are at peace.

I went to a medical doctor and then I was given antidepressants. You see, my case is like this: I was suffering from depression and then year by year that depression was accompanied by a little bit of mania. During winter it's depression, during summer it's mania, and then it was manic depression.

And then I was treated quite nicely in 1988 with the introduction of lithium. It was the third medication that I tried. And now, there is no struggle. Well, there is rain … but there is never a storm.

Lithium is a miracle drug for many sufferers of bipolar disorder. Imagine a remedy for manic episodes that's cheap, has few side effects and is basically a natural product. That's right, natural – lithium is a salt that is mined from the ground, unlike other drugs that are manufactured in a laboratory. And even though it's the oldest medication for treating manic-depressive episodes, it is still generally the first choice of doctors today.

The history of lithium is a story in itself and dates back to Native Americans who sent mentally ill members of their tribe to drink water from lithium springs. It was also an ingredient in the original 7-Up, then called 'Bib-label Lithiated Lemon-Lime Soda'.[55] Sort of rolls off your tongue, doesn't it?

SEASONAL AFFECTIVE DISORDER *OR* WHO TURNED OUT THE LIGHTS?

Seasonal affective disorder, or SAD, is a seasonal depression that strikes in the autumn and abates in the spring each year. For those with the disorder, along with the shortened days of autumn and winter come fatigue, concentration difficulties, irritability, carbohydrate craving, weight gain or loss, and social withdrawal.

Seasonal depression has been around since the time of the ancient Greeks. Back then they recognized how moods and behaviours often changed with the seasons, but it wasn't until the 1980s that SAD was recognized as a 'condition'. To be diagnosed with SAD, your symptoms must begin in mid-October or November, decline in May, and occur over at least two consecutive years.

Although the causes for SAD still are not known, researchers believe that the problem may lie with melatonin, a hormone secreted by the pineal gland that 'brings the body to rest'.[56] Daylight tells the gland to stop producing melatonin, which, in turn, perks us up. The shorter days of winter mean less daylight and more melatonin. It's unclear why some of us are affected by the shorter days and others are not.

The most effective treatment for SAD is to fly somewhere warm and lie on a white, sandy beach for a few days, but if that's not possible, you might want to consider light therapy. Researchers have discovered that sitting 40 cm from a light box for 30 minutes each day can drastically improve the mood of someone with SAD. The standard light box emits 10,000 lux of artificial sunlight, called phototherapy. [57] This light is about 50 times as bright as regular indoor lighting. If light therapy doesn't work, an antidepressant might be prescribed.

It's estimated that more than ten million Americans, the majority of them women, are struck with SAD each year. Phew, that is sad.

DANCING WITH PANIC: THE SWIM

Now if you're under the age of 40, you probably don't remember this dance. But that's all right. The first step of the swim is to float past your panic. Okay, you can stop laughing now. This works, go on – try it. Instead of fight or flight, we'll be choosing float. Panic often strikes in waves: the fear knocks you over, then recedes ever so slightly, then hits you again. If you learn to float with your panic, if you ride it like a wave, it can't knock you over.

During a panic attack

Okay, remember your dance steps? First do the waltz (or breathe), then foxtrot and turn towards your panic, next tango cheek to cheek and embrace your panic, now do the swim and float past your panic. Feel the panic wash over you and then recede. Try to go with it. Don't fight ... float.

AND STILL MORE FUN FACTS TO IMPRESS YOUR FRIENDS

- 20 per cent of people will experience some sort of clinical depression in their lifetime[58]
- Women are two to three times more likely than men to develop depressive illnesses[59]
- Before Terry Bradshaw was diagnosed with clinical depression he led his team, the Pittsburgh Steelers, to eight AFC Central titles and four Super Bowls, in two of which he was the MVP

6 MEDICATIONS *OR* JUST A SPOONFUL OF SUGAR

---

*It was antidepressants, my relationship with my therapist ...
my family and my faith.*[60]

NAOMI JUDD, SINGER AND ACTOR *(on her recovery from panic disorder)*

BEFORE THERE WERE MEDICATIONS, the methods used to treat panic were, well, let's just say they left a little to be desired. If you step back in time a few thousand years, you could expect a surgeon to stretch you out on a wooden table and drill a hole in your skull to 'release the demons within'.[61] As you might imagine, the success rate for this procedure was not high.

Over the centuries, treatment methods didn't improve much. Typically, what we now recognize as anxiety disorders were commonly treated with magic potions, blood-letting, herbal elixirs, even voodoo. Although the treatments have changed considerably, we're still a little bit in the Dark Ages when it comes to a good explanation of how and why antidepressants work. The truth is, scientists just don't know. The good news is, most of the time they do work.

Antidepressants didn't appear until the second half of the twentieth century; that's when things began to change. How that change came about is an interesting tale in itself.[62]

In the 1950s, a group of doctors was searching for a cure for tuberculosis. One remedy that held promise was a drug called iproniazid. Although the drug failed in the treatment of tuberculosis, the researchers noticed that it seemed to have a mood elevation effect on the patients who were taking it. They abandoned their research on iproniazid for the treatment of tuberculosis, but began experimenting with the drug for the treatment of depression.

Actually a lot of scientific discoveries have come about through accidents like this. It happened with penicillin. Apparently Alexander Fleming left a sandwich in his desk drawer before he went on holiday in the summer of 1928. Sure enough, when he came back it was covered with what we like to call 'the fungus among us'. Okay, maybe it wasn't a sandwich, but the point is he wasn't exactly looking for penicillin.

Okay, back to the 1950s. Around that same time another drug, imipramine, was being researched for use in the treatment of psychosis for patients suffering from schizophrenia. Unfortunately this drug was also a failure – as an antipsychotic, that is. The researchers noticed that the imipramine seemed to have an antidepressant effect on the patients taking it. So began the study of antidepressant medication. By the late 1950s, imipramine and iproniazid were marketed in the United States as the first antidepressants.

Over the last four decades, an abundance of research has been conducted with advances being made all the time. A big leap was made in the late 1980s and early 1990s, when government funding allowed scientists to intensify their antidepressant medication research, resulting in better and cleaner medications – medications that are more narrowly or precisely focused, with fewer side effects.

Now most medications have side effects that are experienced by *some* of the people who take them. A few common side effects of the early antidepressant medications included weight gain, dry mouth, and drowsiness. The newer medications have fewer and milder side effects.

Prozac, the first of these new and improved medications, hit the market in 1988. Thousands of people will tell you miraculous recovery stories thanks to this wonder drug. However, it doesn't work for everyone.

Panic diary
Jeanne at age 33
24 February 1990

Dear Diary,
I was in my bedroom, staring at my reflection in a full-length mirror. The sun was streaming in through the window behind me. It felt warm on my back. I studied my reflection. I had lost nearly half of the 15 kilos I had gained while taking the antidepressant imipramine.

After literally a lifetime of panic attacks, one little pill was all it had taken. Amazing. I was so busy enjoying my new state of mind, I had hardly noticed the weight gain at first. Then I kept gaining, and no matter what I did I couldn't lose it.

One day in a friendly conversation with the pharmacist, I

mentioned my sudden weight problem. He told me it was probably due to the imipramine. He said that imipramine was from an older class of medications, and that there were newer antidepressant drugs with fewer side effects.

But I was hesitant. For the first time in my life I wasn't having panic attacks. The mere thought of switching medications caused that familiar flutter in my stomach. But I'm also vain. So I called the doctor. He put me on Prozac and almost immediately I began losing weight. The panic attacks didn't return, so I thought everything was fine.

But then, standing in front of the mirror with the sun on my back, I realized everything wasn't okay. I was sad … very sad. A sadness like I had never really felt before. And as I stood looking in that mirror, I realized something was very wrong.

I went back to the doctor and started on a new antidepressant medication. A few weeks later, no more panic, no more sadness, and no more weight gain. Oh, happy day!

Okay, there was a little dry mouth, but I can live with that.

WHO MOVED MY PROZAC?

So how do antidepressants work, anyway? To answer that, first we have to talk about the nervous system. Think of your nervous system as a big game of dominoes. You start the game with a nerve and each nerve has a receptor. Between each nerve and receptor is a tiny gap called a synapse. Picture a receptor, a nerve and a synapse followed by a receptor, a nerve and a synapse, and so on. Got it?

We'll call the first nerve Biff. Biff releases a chemical into the synapse. That chemical stimulates the receptor on the next nerve; we'll call the next nerve Hal. Biff sends the chemical into the synapse which fires up

Hal's receptor. But then Biff takes a little bit of the chemical back, he reabsorbs it, and what remains in the synapse goes to Hal. So Hal snatches his portion of the chemical, sends it to the next synapse, then he too reabsorbs a little of it himself. All clear so far?

The chemical that Biff and Hal are sending through the system is actually a combination of some powerful stuff: serotonin, epinephrine, norepinephrine, dopamine and a few others. The powerhouse of that combo is the serotonin, which modulates mood, emotion, sleep, appetite, and behaviour. Dopamine, another big guy, regulates movement and emotion. But what these chemicals are really doing is transmitting neural impulses from nerve to nerve, so the chemical is called a neurotransmitter. Clever, isn't it?

Now we can get down to the nitty-gritty of how antidepressant drugs work. There are three categories of antidepressant medication: Tricyclics, MAOIs, and SSRIs. Of these three, the SSRIs are the most frequently prescribed, probably because they're the newest.

Sweet, sweet serotonin

SSRI stands for 'selective serotonin re-uptake inhibitors' (you see why they call them SSRIs). This category includes medications like Prozac (or fluoxetine, which is the generic version of Prozac), paroxetine, sertraline, citalopram and escitalopram. The SSRIs work by increasing the number of neurotransmitters in that little gap called the synapse. But it's not just any neurotransmitter it's increasing, no sir; it selects the serotonin from the neurotransmitter.

That's not all it does. Remember how Biff kept a little of the chemical, the neurotransmitter, for himself? Well, the SSRI stops that hoarding, it inhibits the re-uptake and sends the whole kit and caboodle to

Hal's receptor; hence, 're-uptake inhibitor'. The end result is more serotonin in the synapse, and more serotonin means a happier you. Very cool.

Bring on the GABA

MAOI stands for 'monoamine oxidase inhibitor'. The MAOI category includes the drugs isocarboxazid, phenelzine and tranylcypromine. The MAOIs work by inhibiting monoamine oxidase. You're probably asking, what the heck is monoamine oxidase, anyway? It's an enzyme.

Enzymes are very interesting things. They're like the currency of chemical reactions. It's practically impossible for a chemical reaction to take place without an enzyme. If you can inhibit an enzyme, you can inhibit its effect. Inhibiting monoamine oxidase raises the levels of gamma-aminobutyric acid or GABA, which has a calming effect on the brain. The more GABA you've got, the better you'll feel, which we all know is a good thing.

Lord of the rings

Drugs in the Tricylic category include imipramine, amitriptyline, clomipramine, doxepin and nortriptyline. Imipramine, the first Tricyclic, was studied because of its similarities to the successful antipsychotic drug thorazine. Similar in a chemical way, that is. The Thorazine molecule consisted of three intertwined circular structures called benzene rings. The drug imipramine shares that structure. Tricyclics work by inhibiting the mechanism responsible for the uptake of norepinephrine and serotonin in the nerve cells (think of Biff and Hal), which results in an increased level of neurotransmitters. See, it's all about neurotransmitters. Tricyclics also have the added perk of increasing dopamine levels. The more dopamine, serotonin, and norepinephrine available to your body, the better you feel. It's the three-ringed structure that defines all Tricyclics.[63]

DOCTOR, DOCTOR, GIVE ME THE NEWS

How does your doctor decide what antidepressant to prescribe? According to Dr Mark, it's a combination of factors. 'Most of the time patients take one of the SSRIs. There are many of them, so which one you choose depends on the individual. There are lots of issues, because if someone in your family has had panic attacks and responded well to Prozac, then I'm probably going to prescribe Prozac.'

It's not uncommon to experiment with several medications before hitting on the one that works best. 'Works best' means that the medication greatly reduces or stops symptoms with little or no side effects. 'One of the holy grails of psychiatry is to predict which person is going to respond to which drug,' says Dr Mark. He estimates that he hits on the best medication on the first attempt about two-thirds of the time.

Panic diary
Bridgette at age 45
3 August 1999

Dear Diary,
It was 5:00 a.m. and I was at the airport. I was taking my son to college. We got to the airport too early; I got the times mixed up. So we were first in the queue at Southwest Airlines, which means you're first on the plane. My son was reading this funny letter and we're laughing, we were having a good time … I'm not feeling anxious at all. Not at all.

I start to read a magazine, I'm not nervous or anything, and suddenly I have this physical sensation. It starts right above my navel and goes up to my chest. I feel a jolt, not a mental thing at all; it is totally physical and so intense! It feels as if oxygen and blood are shooting through my body.

I'm thinking, 'What is this? Where is it coming from? It must be a heart attack. I must be dying.' But there is no pain.

I run into the ladies, and I'm thinking, 'Am I dying?' It's just a rush of adrenalin pumping through me and it won't stop. I tell myself if it's a heart attack, if I'm going to die right now, I'll fall down on the ground. But I don't.

Finally I leave the ladies.

So we were the first people in the queue and now we're the last people on the plane. I'm in my seat digging in my purse for the remnants of a 1-milligram Xanax that a girlfriend had given me when I couldn't sleep. It is virtually powder. I am just dipping my finger into this blue powder, thinking that if it calms me down, it's not a heart attack.

We get to my son's college and I take an antacid, which sort of relieves the pressure I'm feeling under my left breast. I still think I'm dying, but I can't tell my son because he's too stressed about leaving his home and friends and starting college.

Later that same day I get on another plane to fly back home, because the following day I happen to be starting a whole new career and I have a class I can't miss. I'm training to become a Pilates instructor. My first child is starting college the day before I begin a major career change.

Once I get home I go to see my doctor. She tells me she thinks it's panic attacks. I tell her, 'I know panic attacks, I had one eight years ago, ended up in casualty, and it was nothing like this.' She puts me on Xanax – half a dose in the morning, half a dose in the afternoon, and a whole one at night. She tells me that I need this straight away, the way I might need an antibiotic. She said, 'You're starting a whole new life now.'

The previous year I had almost died. I made a decision then to change the one thing in my life that I wasn't happy with, my work. I decided to study to become a Pilates instructor. So here I am, going through this struggle and moving through these training classes ... It's like being in a boot camp and I'm the oldest one. I'm just in a sort of daze. But I'm pushing on.

One day I get in the car and I'm on the motorway, on my way to a training class when it hits me again, that same physical sensation. It feels as if a blood clot has broken loose and is racing for my heart or lungs. I don't get it; I wasn't even feeling anxious.

I get off at the nearest exit and head to my doctor's surgery.

She puts me on a heart monitor and runs a round of tests. But my heart is fine.

That physical symptom happened six times in all. But then things changed. The panic didn't start with the physical symptom any more ... it started in my mind.

It felt like I was floating away. And it would build, starting at the bottom and rapidly rising, to the boiling point. It was just all fear, and fear of fear. My own breath scared me to death.

I did everything I could to avoid medication, but it wasn't working. Finally my doctor put me on Prozac, and once it kicked in the panic attacks stopped. I had done some research, and I remembered reading in *Listening to Prozac* about the theory of how your brain gets stuck in a pattern and sometimes only medication can stop it.

I remained on Prozac for two years, before slowly withdrawing. But over those two years I made some changes. I reincorporated other things back into my life, things like yoga and meditation. But when I was lost in panic, those things didn't help me, I needed medicine.

Someone once told me, you can't teach a drowning man to swim, first you've got to toss him a life jacket.

The science of antidepressants is not an exact science. As Dr Charles points out, 'There is no way to draw a serotonin level in your bloodstream and determine you've got low serotonin.' The physician must rely on communication with the patient for the diagnosis and for finding the right medication.

MOTHER'S LITTLE HELPER

Thanks to the Rolling Stones and Jacqueline Susann's titillating novel *Valley of the Dolls*, the world came to know the anti-anxiety medication, Valium. That little yellow pill hit the market in the 1960s and took off running, developing a sort of 'bad girl' image along the way.

Valium is from a family of drugs known as benzodiazepines, which are considered tranquillizers. Before benzodiazepines, barbiturates were the tranquillizers of choice. Drugs like phenobarbital and butabarbital were the barbiturates commonly used to treat anxiety in the early part of the twentieth century, but they had one big drawback – a high rate of addiction to the medication.

The barbiturate family includes more than 2,500 different substances that are used as anti-anxiety drugs, sedatives and anticonvulsants.

They're derived from barbituric acid and act by depressing metabolic functions in several body systems.[64]

Benzodiazepines and barbiturates work much in the same way, by slowing the activity of the central nervous system. However, benzos, as they're sometimes called, do the job with far less toxicity and fewer drug interaction problems than their cousins the barbiturates. Benzos also have a lower risk of cardiovascular and respiratory depression. All and all, they are definitely a better choice.

Valium, or diazepam, which is the generic version of Valium, works like a barbiturate, by slowing the central nervous system. Although Valium was touted as a wonder drug in the 1960s, it did have a few side effects, such as slurred speech and drowsiness, which could be a real problem if you were, say, caring for an infant, or handling a blowtorch, or operating heavy machinery. Newer benzos seem to provide the same anti-anxiety relief as Valium with far fewer side effects.

The fair maiden of the newer benzos is is alprazolam. It was introduced in the 1970s and was approved for the management of anxiety, as well as the treatment of insomnia and depression.

Another favourite, Ativan, or lorazepam, which is the generic version of Ativan, came along a little bit later. It is also similar to Valium, yet considerably milder. In medical terms it has a short half-life, meaning it leaves the system quickly and doesn't produce the 'hangover' effect sometimes common with anti-anxiety medication.[65]

The wonderful thing, the absolutely incredible thing, about benzos is what they can do. For some people that little pill can stop a panic attack dead in its tracks. Now that's some pill.

Panic diary
Julie at age 46
4 January 2004

Dear Diary,
We're halfway through writing this book and I'm in the carpark of a restaurant about to go into a meeting with our editor. I don't do well in restaurants. And I'm not doing so well today. My mother died at Christmas and I'm wading through the grief of her long and difficult death. Truth is, I can barely get around, can barely think about anything, but our deadline's approaching and I've got to make this meeting.

I grab my briefcase and head towards the restaurant door. It's cold outside and it snowed last night and beneath the snow are patches of ice, but I don't see them. Not yet, anyhow. I decide to take an Ativan, probably should have taken one before I left the house – usually I do, and usually it helps – but grief makes you forget about all the usual things.

I grab my prescription bottle from the bottom of my briefcase. It's a new one, just filled a few days ago. My fingers are cold. It's hard to grab a pill, but finally I do. I toss it in my mouth like an anxiety breath mint, then try to put the white cap back on the bottle as I manoeuvre through the clumps of snow.

Next thing I know, I'm slipping on the ice, doing one of those Charlie Chaplin slides. As I try to keep my balance, the pills fly out of the bottle. Each and every one of them. But they don't just fly out, they scatter in a picture-perfect way. And I mean perfect – if it were a film, you'd have to spend a whole day trying to get a shot like that. Three seconds of film, but what a spectacular shot!

I look at the ground in search of my pills. They're hard to see against the white of the snow, but I spot a few of them. My first impulse is to rescue them, to drop to my knees and pluck them from the snow as quickly as I can. But I can see that they're melting. Besides, what am I going to do with 30 wet Ativan tablets? Toss them on the restaurant table and dry them off through the meeting? No. This is just one of those things you walk away from. Nothing left to do here but shake my head and laugh.

Yes, laugh. It's not every day you spill a bottle of anti-anxiety pills on your way into a meeting with the editor of a book on panic!

Although benzos can be a miracle drug for many people, it's important to note that they don't cure panic attacks. They are most frequently used to prevent panic attacks and treat anticipatory anxiety on an as-needed basis. For things like specific phobias that may be enough, but for those struggling with a chronic anxiety disorder, the benzodiazepines are most often used in conjunction with another form of therapy, often with another medical therapy such as antidepressants.

'It takes SSRIs about four weeks to work,' says Dr Mark, 'so I'll often give a patient a benzo too, and they get relief the same day and they love you. I'd say most of the time I take people off the benzos at least within two months, but occasionally someone will stay on longer.'

Benzos are also used within certain cognitive and behavior therapies, most frequently exposure therapy. The benzodiazepines reduce the patient's symptoms of anxiety, allowing them to achieve a higher level of exposure in their therapy.

Medication isn't the only option when it comes to the treatment of anxiety disorders. There are other treatments available – some more conventional than others. In the next chapter, we'll take a little tour through the various treatments out there today.

DANCING WITH PANIC: THE POLKA

The final dance step in our series is the panic polka. The polka is a dance full of energy and joy, full of spinning and kicking up of the heels. It's hard to polka without a smile. And the polka is a dance of individuality: whether you're reserved or flamboyant, each person brings their own unique style to the dance floor.

The polka is a dance of commitment and trust, all of the things that are vital to a recovery. So practise your dance steps, smile, kick up your heels, trust in yourself and, occasionally ... spin!

MORE FUN FACTS TO IMPRESS AND AMAZE YOUR FRIENDS

- In 1999, approximately 135 million prescriptions were written in the US for antidepressants[66]
- A significant number of people who are prescribed antidepressants are not technically depressed
- People taking MAOIs must avoid pickled herring, liver, and sauerkraut (which may be a good enough reason for taking MAOIs!)[67]

- *Valley of the Dolls*, which was first published in 1966, is a title that passed into American vernacular to describe addiction to prescription drugs[68]

7 FOLLOW THE YELLOW BRICK ROAD TO RECOVERY

Pay no attention to the man behind the curtain.

THE GREAT AND POWERFUL WIZARD OF OZ

EMEMBER THE RUBY SLIPPERS? How do you think Dorothy felt when she discovered that she really didn't have to hike through a forest with some seriously hostile apple trees or get locked in that draughty castle with a nasty green witch and those creepy flying monkeys ... well, let's not even go there. Turns out that all she had to do was click her heels together three times and say those five little words, 'There's no place like home.' Who knew? She went through all of that turmoil for nothing. Well, maybe not nothing. She made a few good friends along the way (although we found the Tin Man a little distant). She discovered who she was and what was really important in her life. Although she was in distress, she was experiencing personal growth, and that's always a good thing.

The point is, even if you have the power, it might take a while to get where you want to be. And yes, recovery from panic attacks can be like trying to get out of Oz. But with hard work, chances are you'll succeed.

What does recovery mean, exactly? Let's consult the dictionary.[69]

Recovery: the act or power of regaining, retaking or conquering again.

Conquering sounds too much like fighting, usually not a good idea with panic.

Recovery: a getting well again, coming or bringing back to consciousness, revival of a person from weakness.

Okay, that's better.

Recovery: a return to soundness.

Ahhh, there you go.

Notice that it doesn't say, 'never has another recurrence'. So what does recovery mean in relation to panic attacks? In an attempt to get to the bottom of this, we took the stairs to the basement. (Just kidding.) We asked our experts.

'A lot of studies define recovery as a certain percentage of a decrease of symptoms,' said Dr Mark, 'not complete relief. But that said, most people experience a dramatic reduction in their symptoms, maybe 90 per cent. I think most people say that recovery means I am able to do most of the things I want to do.'

Our other expert, Dr Charles, says, 'Probably the best definition of recovery would be being able to maintain a normal level of functioning in a social setting, meaning being able to work, able to go to family functions, able to live life without impairment.'

Recovery is an individual issue. One person's recovery may mean they never have another panic attack, another's may mean they have an attack only once a month, yet both consider themselves recovered.

Panic diary
Jenna Glatzer at age 27
15 April 2003

Dear Diary,
It was a good day. Not so long ago, I couldn't make it as far as my gate, but today, I got up enough nerve to go to the shops and look for a dress for my forthcoming class reunion. I was going to make it there, no matter how many panic attacks tried to stop me. And I was going to wear something pretty.

While I was looking through the racks, an old friend spotted me. We hadn't seen each other for years, so of course she wanted to catch up. The only problem was that the second she opened her mouth, my brain exploded. Suddenly, everything was too loud and dreamlike and out of proportion, and her voice sounded like the teacher in the Charlie Brown cartoons. I withstood it as long as I could, nodding and fighting facial tics and nausea, but eventually, the dizziness overcame me. I dropped to the floor.

I clutched a dress rack stand and sat there and forced a smile, pretending I was just casually sitting, though we both knew otherwise. She didn't let on that she thought I had gone insane, but I was terrified. I had no idea how I was going to get out of the shopping centre and now I was sprawled out on the floor, unable to speak, certain a brain tumour was rupturing.

> She left. I hid behind dresses until I could compose myself
> enough to stand and force my heart to stop going off like a
> machine gun in my chest. I made it out to the car. It was a
> good day.

Sometimes recovery is not what you think it is. The scarecrow wanted a brain, but he got a diploma. The cowardly lion wanted courage and he got a medal. So they didn't exactly get what they wanted, but they did get tools to help them find their way.

In order to help you find your way, we've gathered together a cornucopia of treatments and therapies. Some you've heard of, some you probably haven't. Some will require a therapist or a teacher, while others won't. But they all have one thing in common: they helped somebody recover.

PSYCHOTHERAPY *OR* TALK TO ME

Psychotherapy is basically talk therapy, and yes, you will do most of the talking. In psychotherapy you meet with a trained therapist, usually once or twice a week, where you discuss different problems you might be experiencing. By listening carefully to what you say and through his or her own expertise, a therapist can help you identify self-destructive patterns in your life or recognize suppressed feelings, then help you learn to express yourself in a healthier way.

Some therapists concentrate primarily on your childhood and identifying emotional problems related to your upbringing. A childhood trauma may be causing a problem; perhaps your parents divorced when you were five, or ... well, there are a lot of possibilities here. Psychotherapy doesn't necessarily stop panic attacks, but it can help to reduce anxiety and overall stress, which are directly linked to panic attacks. The benefits of psychotherapy don't stop there: it can also improve your relationships and help you to get in touch with your own feelings.

COGNITIVE THERAPY *OR* IF I ONLY HAD A BRAIN

'Cognitive' refers to your thinking process. Cognition represents the voice in your head and the images in your mind. What happens when that voice and those images perceive the events in the world and in your life in a distorted manner?

Let's say you get a headache, a particularly bad headache. If you're a panicker, you might immediately think that the headache is a brain aneurysm. Someone who is not a panicker might think, 'I bet I'm getting Perry's head cold,' or 'This must be a premenstrual headache,' or 'The stress of buying that house is really getting to me.' Then they would probably take an aspirin. But a panicker might have the distorted thought of an aneurysm, which kickstarts the whole cycle of fear. Distorted thoughts can pop up when you least expect them: driving a car, hearing an ambulance siren, or on holiday at a beautiful resort.

Panic diary
Maurice at age 26
23 April 1982

Dear Diary,
Several years ago my wife and I took a wonderful holiday in Puerta Vallarta, Mexico. We were staying at a beautiful resort, but my wife wanted to take an excursion away from the resort, to really see the place. So we asked around and we found a

man named Jesus Flores, who takes people on tours of the area on horseback.

He meets us very early with two horses and we set off on our journey. We head away from the resort, out of the tourist area, and up into the hills. Just outside of the town there is a river that empties into the Pacific Ocean. We followed this river, first through some small towns, then farther away from the coast. We saw terrible poverty – families living in corrugated tin roof homes with no pipes or running water. It was quite educational for my wife and me. But our guide kept going and we got even further out, into a forested area. And all through this ride, the thought that keeps going through my head is, 'This guy is going to take us into the hills and kill us.' My wife is absolutely enjoying herself, totally absorbed in the natural beauty of the area. And me, I'm preparing to die.

We're going on and on and I'm getting more and more panicked. I take a Valium, and I suggest that we turn round, but I'm told, 'Just a little bit further.' And then our guide takes us to this desolate area and tells us to dismount, tells us that we're going to rest the horses before our journey back.

And that's it for me, I'm thinking, 'Okay, this is it, this is the end, we're going to die now. The banditos are going to come from the hills, they're going to steal our money and slit our throats.' My heart is pounding out of my chest. Nobody knows where we are. I am just terrified. I am seeing full-blown images of blood splattering, of my wife and me being brutally murdered. Then our guide climbed back on his horse. And so did we. We turned the horses and started the journey back to our hotel. It wasn't long before I realized we were safe.

I saved his business card. It's in my scrapbook.

Cognitive therapy teaches you, with the help of a therapist, how to change that thought process by first recognizing the distorted thoughts and then changing them to more positive and realistic thoughts.

Cognitive therapy was developed more than 30 years ago by Dr Aaron T. Beck at the Beck Institute for Cognitive Therapy and Research in Philadelphia.[70] The programme consists of ten principles or steps for recovery. It's important that the therapist you choose be trained in this specific discipline.

BEHAVIOUR THERAPY *OR* IF I ONLY HAD A BIGGER BRAIN

In 1955, Dr Albert Ellis developed a mode of therapy called REBT, which stands for rational-emotive behaviour therapy.[71] REBT was the first form of behavior therapy and it took patients off the couch and offered them a therapeutic approach in response to their fears. The theory behind REBT is replacing self-defeating thoughts, feelings and actions with positive and effective ones.

Although REBT is still used, most behaviour therapists today concentrate their treatment on the symptoms of anxiety rather than the unconscious conflicts that might cause such symptoms.[72] The goal of behaviour therapy is to modify the behaviour response to certain thoughts that produce anxiety. Behavioural techniques teach a patient to take control at a time when they feel out of control. There are several types of behaviour techniques that fall under the heading of behaviour therapy, including exposure therapy, visualization, meditation and biofeedback; we'll cover them in this chapter.

The most commonly used treatment today is a combination of cognitive and behaviour therapy, creatively called cognitive-behaviour therapy, or CBT. CBT seems to offer the best of both worlds. Cognitive therapy works to modify or eliminate certain thought patterns, while behaviour therapy attempts to change actual behaviour responses.[73] Seems like a good plan. Typically a CBT patient meets with a therapist one to three hours per week, with the duration of therapy fairly short, usually about three months.[74]

The National Institute of Mental Health states that CBT can bring significant relief to 70 to 90 per cent of people with panic disorder. Those are some pretty sweet numbers.

BIOFEEDBACK *OR* IT'S WHAT'S INSIDE THAT COUNTS

Biofeedback is just what it sounds like – the feedback of biological information. Biofeedback is a therapy performed by a psychotherapist or doctor trained in this particular technique. It involves practising different types of relaxation techniques while you are hooked up to electrodes attached to your fingers, neck or forehead. It's all quite painless and, since many panickers are goal-oriented type-A personalities, they respond well to performance testing.[75]

These electrodes record certain information such as heart rate, skin temperature, perspiration and muscle tension, as the data travel from the electrodes to a computer. Through the miracle of modern technology, the patient can see inside his body, or to be more specific, he can see the information that corresponds to what's going on inside his body.

This is quite fun in and of itself, but it gets better. By practising the relaxation techniques, a patient can 'see' his heart and respiratory rates go down. Or up. Biofeedback takes the guesswork out of what's happening in your body. After enough practice, you don't need those electrodes any more to tell you what's going on inside. After enough practice with the relaxation techniques, you can learn to control your breathing, which in turn controls your heart rate, which in turn controls ... you get the idea.

Biofeedback allows you to see your progress, even if it's small, and a lot of people find this experience empowering.

HYPNOSIS *OR* SHALL WE TRANCE?

The first medical use of hypnosis was introduced by Franz Anton Mesmer (1734–1815), an Austrian physician. If you've ever been mesmerized, you have Dr Mesmer to thank. (Thank you, Dr Mesmer!)

Although the exact mechanisms aren't completely understood, current research suggests that hypnosis can trick the brain into registering something as real.[76] In fact, brain scans of hypnotized individuals show 'they actually perceive what they are told is reality even when it clearly is not.'[77] The American Society of Clinical Hypnosis defines hypnosis as 'a state of inner absorption, concentration and focused attention',[78] similar to when you drive your car to the shops and have no memory of getting there.

During hypnosis the focus of the mind in the hypnotic state makes it very receptive to creating a believable reality. By harnessing the power of the hypnotic state, a person can create new responses to the things that trigger their anxiety. Many hypnotherapists believe anxiety can be viewed as the subconscious mind trying to communicate. Christopher Bathum, a Californian hypnotherapist who treats anxiety and phobias, teaches people to listen to what their anxiety is telling them. He uses hypnosis to foster an 'integration between the mind and heart or between consciousness and the subconscious mind'.

Hypnosis can also be used to achieve a state of inner calm and relaxation that can help to diminish the physical symptoms of anxiety. Hypnotherapy doesn't work for everyone, but it doesn't take long to discover if it will work for you.

EXPOSURE THERAPY *OR* PUT ONE LOOK IN FRONT OF THE OTHER

Exposure therapy is a form of CBT that 'emerged in response to the need for more intensive, direct, and effective interventions for crippling anxiety and stress disorders'.[79] In other words, exposure therapy was created especially for people like us!

The basic premise of exposure therapy is that a person's anxiety or phobia can be diminished by exposing the person to anxiety-provoking stimuli.

It's not as scary as it sounds. The goal of exposure therapy is for a person to build up a tolerance to the feared object, place or situation and to reframe or recondition the response. In other words, exposure therapy is relearning how to react to a particular stimulus. You might compare it to taking allergy injections in order to build up your tolerance to pollen or animal fur.

In addition to exposing a person to controlled doses of the fear-provoking stimulus, exposure therapy alters the person's fearful response by providing a safe environment in which to experience the fear and by surrounding the 'anxiety moments' with positive experiences.

Let's say you have an intense fear of doorknobs, but you adore kittens and puppies. Your therapist might put together a series of 31 pictures for you to look at. The first 15 are all cosy kittens and snuggly puppies.

You're feeling all warm inside, relaxed and soothed. Now comes the 16th picture; it's a doorknob. You feel a flash of doorknob panic. It doesn't feel good, but here come the kittens again, here come the adorable little puppies.

Next time around, it's two doorknobs, two flashes of doorknob anxiety. But the negative experience of anxiety is padded by the positive experiences of all those kittens and puppies. Over time, the positive feelings you associate with those furry friends will recondition the way you feel about doorknobs. In fact, following a basic premise of behaviour theory, you might even get to the point where seeing a doorknob will be as positive an experience as seeing a puppy!

Until recently, exposure therapy was done either *in vitro* or *in vivo*. *In vitro* exposure is also called imaginal exposure and this involves the therapist helping the client to imagine the anxiety-provoking stimuli. *In vivo* exposure is actual exposure to the feared object or situation or event. If you're afraid of lifts or spiders or tall buildings, *in vivo* exposure therapy will involve actual experience in a lift, with a spider, or near a tall building. As you might imagine, *in vivo* exposure therapy presents several obstacles. Not every therapist will meet you in a lift or on the roof of a tall building. And although we don't know any personally, we've heard that some therapists actually have a strict 'no-spiders-allowed' policy.

VIRTUAL REALITY *OR* TRON, TRON, TRON

A third and relatively new exposure therapy is called virtual reality, or VR, exposure. VR is a human-computer interaction paradigm in which subjects are 'exposed' to the feared object by 'entering' the virtual world of a software program. One such program is called Spiderworld.[80] It was created by Hunter Hoffman of the Human Interface Technology

Laboratory at the University of Washington, and Al Carlin, a therapist who had a client with a debilitating fear of spiders. The client completely overcame her fear of spiders and later appeared in *Spiders*, a Scientific American Frontiers programme on PBS, holding a cute, fuzzy tarantula in the palm of her hands.

At present there are VR programs available for fear of flying, rats, snakes, spiders, driving, public speaking, thunderstorms, and for claustrophobia. There's even one for panic disorder with agoraphobia where a person can 'practise' being in a shopping cenre, a restaurant, an office, or a square. One of the key benefits of VR exposure therapy is that the individual is able to control the anxiety-provoking stimuli.

Although it is one of the newer therapies available, controlled studies have shown that people who opt for exposure therapy have a 92 per cent chance of substantial recovery. Dr Brenda Weiderhold, Executive Director of the Virtual Reality Medical Center in San Diego, California, believes that 'VR holds great promise for those that haven't been able to overcome their fears with traditional therapy because it puts people in control.' Dr Weiderhold has treated more than four hundred patients with a combination of VR and biofeedback. A follow-up study of individuals who used this combination for fear of flying had almost no recurrence. Because their therapy addressed the cognitive as well as the physical – the mind and the body – these individuals were 'quicker to catch their anxiety' and 'less frightened of the physical symptoms'. Although it's not yet available at the corner shop, there are several VR centres in America and Europe.

EMDR *OR* SWEET DREAMS ARE MADE OF THESE
Eye movement desensitization and reprocessing, or EMDR, was developed in America by Dr Francine Shapiro in the mid-1990s. EMDR

is an 'information processing therapy' that integrates elements of cognitive behaviour, interpersonal, experiential, and body-centered therapies.[81]

During an EMDR session, the therapist moves her fingers back and forth across the client's field of vision. While this is happening, the client focuses on an image or thought that has been previously targeted as an unprocessed or inadequately processed memory or trauma or negative event. The therapist stops her hand movements and the client is encouraged to free-associate and just notice whatever thoughts or feelings or sensations come to mind. This process is repeated several times throughout a session. The goal is for the therapist's hand movements to cause the client's eyes to move the way they do during REM sleep. It's akin to tricking the brain into thinking it's dreaming, or into behaving somewhat like it does in a dream.

While there are many different theories about the nature and purpose of dreams, it's generally agreed that dreams are one way in which the brain processes information. Dr Robert Stickgold, a psychiatrist at Harvard Medical School, has suggested that dreams 'have evolved to provide a privileged time during which the brain/mind is optimally tuned for memory transfer and integration'.[82]

Certain anxiety disorders, especially PTSD, can be seen as the inability of the brain to properly process and store information. By targeting memories and sensations that are associated with traumatic events, EMDR creates an occasion for the brain/mind to process the information attached to these events.

More than 60,000 people have been treated with EMDR and it has been approved as an effective treatment for PTSD by the American

Psychological Association and the International Society for Traumatic Stress Studies.

EAST MEETS WEST MEETS ...

Not all treatments are created equal. Treatments or therapies with a professional are generally short-term. But other treatments can involve lifestyle changes. These treatments rely on a commitment to regular practice for the promised rewards.

Meditation *or* Stop the chatter

There are many styles of meditation, too many to list here; however, what they all share is a remedy for mind, body and spirit.[83] The practice of meditation is an art that originated from the Eastern religious practices of China, Japan and India more than 5,000 years ago. Traditionally, meditation was a spiritual practice; however, in the 1960s an Indian leader, Maharishi Majesh Yogi, introduced Transcendental Meditation, or TM, to the Western world.

TM is performed by silently reciting a mantra, which is a simple word or sound, over and over again while sitting in a quiet place. The practice of TM became quite popular with the flower children and the jetsetters of the 1960s generation. Then in 1968, Herbert Benson, a Harvard cardiologist, researched TM. His findings were remarkable. He discovered that the regular practice of TM resulted in a decrease in heart rate, blood pressure, cholesterol levels and oxygen consumption, as well as a decrease in the concentration of lactic acid in the blood (associated with anxiety reduction). He also noted increases in blood flow and alpha brain-wave activity, as well as an increased energy level. Other perks include increased longevity and heightened self-esteem. You can bet that if there were a pill that provided these results, everyone would be taking it.

Benson also studied Hindu and Buddhist meditation techniques and concluded that these extraordinary health benefits were not exclusive to TM, but included all types of meditation.[84] He continued his research and finally developed his own style, a combination of meditation and yoga, which he called the Relaxation Response. This practice style combines breathing exercises and progressive relaxation.[85]

Research shows that most people who meditate feel less anxious and more in control of their lives. Regular practice can also help heal old traumas, allow forgiveness, or even help one confront and embrace a strong fear of death.[86] So why doesn't everyone meditate?

Yoga *or ...* Yoga

Yoga is an ancient practice, first described in detail in the third century BC. The word *yoga* means 'unity' or 'oneness'. It signifies the unity of mind and body as well as individual unity to everyone and everything. There are different styles of yoga; however, the most common in the Western world is Hatha Yoga.

The word *hatha* is derived from *ha* and *tha*, which are symbols for the sun and the moon. Hatha signifies the positive and negative forces of the universe in the electromagnetic sense.[87] It also signifies balance, which is the true lesson of yoga. Balance is essential in all aspects of your life – in what you eat and drink, in your work and play, in your sexual life, and even in your practice of yoga.

To practise yoga you hold your body in specific positions, each known as an asana. Each asana also has its own name related to the form or position itself. The asanas range from simple to quite advanced and difficult. Holding a pose or an asana is only the first part of yoga practice. The second part is breathing, and not your regular, everyday, run-of-the-mill breathing. It's a special breathing technique known as pranayama.[88] The combination of the asana and the pranayama practices make up yoga.

For the last 25 years, Dr Dean Ornish at the Preventative Medicine Research Institute has been researching, among other things, the effects of a disciplined yoga practice. The results of his study revealed that practising yoga regularly, as part of a healthy lifestyle, contributed to reversal of the symptoms of heart disease over a 12-month period.[89]

Yoga is the practice of mindfulness, or steadiness of the mind – being absolutely present as you practise each pose. It's this very steadiness of the mind and balance of energy that allows you to achieve new levels of relaxation, which in turn can reduce feelings of anxiety.

Tai Chi *or* The action of non-action

Tai Chi is an exercise technique sometimes described as a 'meditation in movement'. In China it's not unusual to see hundreds of people crowded into a park practising expansive, slow, dance-like moves. This series of fluid and graceful movements, known as Tai Chi, brings the body into a harmonious rhythm, which increases one's vitality.[90] The art of Tai Chi is thought to be at least 5,000 years old, dating back to the time of the Chinese Emperor Fu His. Tai Chi is represented by the well-known circle divided into two teardrops, one light, one dark (the Yin and the Yang), which represent opposites, such as good and bad, male and female, day and night, and many more. But the goal is not opposites, but the unity of all things and the belief that you cannot know one without the other. Tai Chi classes are now offered at many hospitals and leisure centres, often as a way to reduce stress and anxiety. Tai Chi is commonly practised in the early morning hours in the hopes of achieving a more centred and relaxed day. [91]

Exercise *or* Just do it!

Talk about your ruby slippers ... how about ruby running shoes? The physical and mental benefits of a regular exercise programme are simply astounding. Research shows vigorous, regular exercise can reduce tension as well as cholesterol levels, pH levels, and blood pressure. Just wait until you hear what it improves. How about circulation, blood sugar levels, concentration and memory, as well as self-esteem? And that's just a few. Then there are the endorphins, the natural chemicals that increase your overall sense of well-being. No wonder exercise is fast becoming part of treatment plans prescribed by many doctors and therapists as one of the most powerful and effective methods for reducing anxiety and panic attacks.[92]

But exercise doesn't just mean walking your dog, or taking the stairs instead of the lift; although these are both good choices, they're not enough. Regular exercise means just that: exercise done on a regular basis. Ideally it should be aerobic exercise – running, walking, or biking – or anything that increases your heart rate for 20 to 30 minutes or more per session. There are formulas and charts available to determine your own target heart rate; however, a good general rule is that you need to sweat. To achieve the results mentioned, you'll need to work out four to five days per week.

If you're like most people, you have many good reasons why you can't possibly exercise. You don't have the time, you can't afford a health club, you're too old, you can't leave the house .... But you can achieve results with as little as two and a half hours per week. You can walk or run around your block or do yoga or Tai Chi in your basement. If you think your health prohibits you from working out, talk to your doctor first, then just do it!

IF YOU GET LEMONS, MAKE LEMONADE ... *OR* MARGARITAS

Recovery can take all forms. For some people, the road is quick and straightforward. For others, it might be hairpin bends with no safety barriers. And sometimes it's just a bumpy road, heading where you'd least expect it.

Panic diary
Amy at age 43
19 January 2004

I have dealt with anxiety/panic disorder for approximately 20 years. However, one night in particular stands out in my mind more than any other.

Most of my panic attacks occur at night and that one was no exception. I had only been experiencing panic attacks for a couple of months by then, but neither my regular doctor nor those at the casualty department could tell me what was happening. They all said they could not find anything wrong with me.

That night, in bed, I noticed my heart beat faster than normal. I was certain something was wrong. I jumped out of bed, ran to the living room and within seconds I was in a full-blown panic attack. It felt as though the room was spinning out of control. For the first several minutes I was cold, and then I began to sweat. My heart raced so fast I could barely tell one beat from the next. Although I did not know it at the time, I was experiencing almost every single one of the classic symptoms of a panic attack all at once. I was dizzy, nauseous, and I knew I was going to die. I wanted help, but I had gone to casualty so many times, I was now too embarrassed to return.

My agony went on for hours. It would ease up for a short time and then come back even stronger. Finally, around four o'clock in the morning, exhaustion had made me desperate enough to look for my doctor's home number in the phone book. I found it and decided to call just to see if he would believe me this time. The phone rang several times before he finally answered. I began to cry and pour out my soul to him. I wanted more than anything to hear him acknowledge that there was something wrong with me. Certainly this time he would be able to diagnose the source of my racing heart. He would have to know what caused the room to spin.

Ultimately, however, I received just the opposite, as this man – my doctor, for goodness' sake – yelled at me over the phone.

'There is nothing wrong with you,' he said, 'and do not ever call me at home again.' Then he hung up. It was the worst night of my life.

Years passed as I suffered in silence. How could it be that nothing was wrong with me? I knew without a doubt that something was wrong, but if my doctor couldn't see it, what hope did I have?

One day, however, I came to learn that my experience actually had a name and that I wasn't alone. From then on, my goal in life was to share my experiences with others so no one else would ever have to unnecessarily feel the loneliness, doubt and fear I had endured. That goal has been realized through my website – anxietypanic.com.

DANCING WITH PANIC: THE HOKEY-POKEY

Okay, it's not really a technique, but then again it's not really a dance either, it's a riddle. But since this entire chapter is like one giant technique, we thought we'd give you a break. So we put together a word scramble.

Below is a phrase that appears in this chapter. Unscramble the letters and then the words to reveal the phrase. When you've finished you can check your answers on page 147. Here's a hint: could have been tarmac.

CIKRB

LEWYOL

HET

ADOR

LWOOFL

JUST A FEW MORE ASTONISHING FUN FACTS

- In the 1600s, French farmers learnt to hypnotize hens to sit on other hen's eggs. (We think there was probably some wine involved with this ...)
- The phrase 'animal magnetism' comes from Mesmer's ideas that the air we breathe is filled with magnetic particles
- The word *hypnosis* comes from the Greek word *ypnos*, meaning 'sleep or trance'

8 THE LYIN' KING

*The face is the mirror of the mind, and eyes without
speaking confess the secrets of the heart.*

SAINT JEROME

PANIC ATTACKS CAN BE SCARY to talk about. Scary for a lot of reasons. First and foremost, you don't know how people will react to your admission. Will they laugh at you or be afraid of you? Will they think you're crazy? And what about your boss: will you lose your job? What about your spouse: will they stick around for this? What about your friends: will they still call?

So, yeah, it's all big-time scary stuff ... we know that. But talking about your panic attacks is an essential step on the road to recovery. You need to throw open the doors and step out of the closet. Go to the doctor, talk to your family, go to the library, do research, read, write, sing ... well, maybe not sing. But the point is to move forward.

And here's another important point: panic attacks generally don't just go away on their own. They're not like a cold or the flu. Panic attacks don't simply run their course and disappear. Left untreated, panic attacks or any anxiety disorder will most likely progress and get worse over time.

SEX, LIES, AND INSULATING TAPE *OR* HOW TO TALK TO YOUR PARTNER

Most likely your partner is already aware that something is wrong if you're struggling with panic, but just being aware isn't enough. It's important that your partner understands as much as possible about your anxiety disorder and the symptoms of your disorder. In a loving relationship, a partner will certainly try to be supportive, but it's very difficult for someone who has not experienced a panic attack to truly understand it. How does a woman understand how the man she has built a life with, that she has laughed with and slept beside for the past five years, is suddenly afraid to drive to work? How does a man understand how the woman he has shared his dreams with, raised children with, and depended on for the last seven years, is suddenly unable to go into a grocery store or the cleaners or a bank?

Panic is tough on a partner. Agreed, it's no picnic for the panicker, either. Feeling alienated from the person you're closest to can make it nearly impossible for you to have a 'normal' relationship. Sometimes a partner may become your 'safe' person: the only person with whom you can go in a car or attend a social function or, eventually, the only person with whom you can leave the house. This arrangement of over-reliance drastically alters the natural husband and wife relationship and can become a terrible burden for the partner of the panicker.[93]

Sometimes the panicker grows complacent with this arrangement and loses the motivation to challenge himself or work towards recovery. Even if your partner loves you deeply, caring for someone with panic disorder for an extended period of time can be an extremely difficult task, causing the relationship to degenerate and sometimes end.

A partner needs encouragement and support as much as the panicker they love. They also need information. A lack of knowledge about anxiety disorders can lead to tension and criticism in the relationship, which can hinder your recovery process.

Panic diary
Stephanie at age 31
27 June 2003

Dear Diary,
It's happening again – I have to leave the room. I can feel it rising inside me, starting in my gut, closing off the air to my lungs, swelling into my throat. I tell my husband I am going to have a shower and get ready for bed.

He looks at me strangely. I smile and walk out of the room.

I hurry to get into the shower, my sanctuary. In here, I can give in to the panic, give into the fear. I can cry and he won't know, he won't hear. He won't look at me with worry and sadness in his eyes. I just cry and cry and cry and try to breathe.

Finally, the panic begins to relent, it begins to subside, and I try to find the trigger. What was it this time? Oh, yes – my husband wants to go out with new friends this weekend.

Great, new people, a new place, another opportunity to try to appear normal.

And then, I feel the guilt. We live near one of the greatest cities in the States and all I want to do is stay at home. The thought of leaving the flat sends fear racing through my body. It is hard enough to leave for work every day, but then to go out at the weekend?

> As I stand in the shower thinking about it, the exhaustion sets in. All I want to do is go to bed. I have two days to prepare, two days to find the courage, two days to fight the fear, two days to fight the panic, two days to convince myself not to cancel. I can't disappoint him again.

Disappointment. Guilt. How do you help a partner understand panic? Probably the best strategy is for your partner to be directly involved in your treatment. Involvement begins by discussing your anxieties openly with your partner. Many panickers 'manage' their avoidance behaviours for a long time, usually through the smoke and mirrors of excuses – excuses like 'I just don't feel like going to a restaurant', or 'I was busy and I couldn't make it to the shops.' These white lies can take a toll on a relationship.

The first step is to open up, talk to your partner, and then include him or her in your recovery process. Often your partner can benefit from a few visits to your therapist as well. You can get through this, but it will require patience on the part of your partner and, just as important, your partner must feel confident about your commitment to recovery.

Panic diary
Jeanne at age 32
8 July 1989

Dear Diary,
The car is packed. My husband slams the boot, gives it an extra push. The kids tumble over each other scrambling into the

back seat. They're loud. They're excited. It's time to go.

My in-laws have a summer house on a lake, about two hundred miles from our home. They have a boat, water skis and rubber rings – all the makings of a great family holiday. They've had the place for four years, but this is only our second trip. The first trip is still etched vividly in my mind. It wasn't good – not for me, anyway.

My in-laws don't understand why we don't come. My husband tries to explain it to them, but I don't think they get it. I'm sure they're hurt. They think I don't want to be with them, that I can't feel comfortable or safe in their home. I hate it that I make them feel bad; I hate that my children miss out because of me. So this year I decided we were going.

I made the announcement. Heard the joy in my father-in-law's voice, felt it right through the telephone line. Watched my children literally leap with joy. Listened to them plan and talk about it, their eyes lit up with expectation.

I, on the other hand, haven't felt so great. It's all I think about. For the last four weeks I've been obsessed with the prospect of this trip. Counting down the days as they get closer. Not sleeping at night. Not concentrating during the day. Knowing that all too soon it would be here, and I would have to go. There is no way out.

I grab my bag and stand in the doorway. They're all in the car, waiting. Finally I'm in the car, the window's rolled down, I feel the wind in my face. Then we're on the highway, everyone's excited … everyone except me. Then we're on the motorway and traffic is heavy and slow. I can feel the pressure of anxiety pushing against my throat, choking me.

The kids are fighting in the back seat. They're getting

louder, but I don't do anything; I can't because everything I have is being used up at the moment. Everything I have is going towards breathing and not shrieking at the top of my lungs and not leaping from this moving car. And, above all, hiding every bit of it from my three children. I glance over at my husband. He's looking at me. He tries so hard to understand, to help me, but he really doesn't get it. He doesn't understand why I can't be a parent at this moment when he really needs me to be.

And then I catch it – that look in his eyes. It's only for a fleeting second; if I hadn't looked at just that moment I wouldn't have seen it, but I did. And there it was – disappointment.

My husband handles the problems in the back seat and the kids settle down. Soon all three are asleep. We're off the motorway and on an open country road. The sun sparkles through a canopy of trees. It's beautiful. I feel a little better.

Only four days left.

MUMMY DEAREST *OR* WHAT DO I TELL MY KIDS?

This is a tough one. Your children depend on you to take care of them. Simply blurting out that you can't take them roller-skating because you might have a panic attack and pass out in the middle of the rink probably isn't the best idea. There is no definitive answer about how much or how little information you should offer your child about your anxiety disorder. However, something to consider before having that conversation is the level of your child's anxiety. Remember, panic can have a genetic component, sometimes referred to as the 'worry gene'.[94] Anxious parents often have anxious children, so you don't want to bombard them with facts and symptoms that might scare them.

Often the gauge for how much to say will come from your child. In the beginning, offer small amounts of non-specific information. Generally, the fewer details you offer, the less your child will worry about you. Try to measure her initial response, then let her ask you questions. Listen carefully to those questions. If your child continues to ask questions, she needs more information. When the questions stop, your child is probably satisfied with your explanation. Remember, of course, to consider the age of your child. A 15-year-old will have more understanding than an eight-year-old.

How you convey the information is just as important as what you say. Try to be calm and reassuring when you explain your symptoms and talk about your recovery.

TAKE THIS JOB AND ... FIND ME ANOTHER ONE, QUICK!

Should you tell your boss or colleagues about your anxiety disorder? No one can answer that question but you. However, what we can do is give you some very pertinent information on the subject. Okay, the bottom line is ... we've got good news and bad news. Let's start with the bad news.

Research suggests that people are more comfortable working with someone who is physically disabled than someone with a psychiatric disability. Ignorance of anxiety disorders is a real problem here. Often your boss and co-workers will begin to treat you differently once they are aware of your situation. Many employers associate the potential for violence with anyone having a psychiatric disorder.[95] Small companies can be more understanding than large corporations, but still the risk an unfavourable response can be high.

Now for the good news. The Disability Discrimation Act of 1995 was enacted to protect the rights of individuals with disabilities. Believe it or not, this probably includes you. We highly recommend reading this document and understanding your legal rights in the workplace before disclosing your disorder to your employer.

JULIE AND JEANNE

Speaking of disclosure ... Remember we promised to share our individual stories with you? Although we have written this book with one voice, you'll notice our stories are quite different. Here they are.

Panic diary
Julie at age 46
20 February 2004

Dear Diary,
This is the part where I'm supposed to tell the story of my personal struggle with panic and anxiety. Jeanne and I have written five screenplays together, and I know that the best way to tell a story is to know how it ends. But as far as panic and anxiety are concerned, I'm in the middle of my story. I don't know how it ends.

I feel awkward about this. At least I did at first, but then it occurred to me that many who read this book might also be in the middle of their stories. And that's part of the purpose of this book – to speak out and tell the truth so that others might feel less alone.

My own story has been complicated by what has been, as they say, a very bad year for me. I watched my mother fight a horrible battle with cancer only to see her die on Christmas Day. That was just over six weeks ago. And just yesterday, the phone rang early in the morning with news of another death – my mother's sister had died suddenly in the night. So here I am, looking back at my struggle with panic and laying out funeral clothes.

My struggle began when I was three years old. I experienced a violent and disturbing event that filled me with terror. I cannot tell you about this experience; all I can tell you is that it is my first memory and, for whatever reason, I simply never told anyone (okay, so it's probably not simple, but I don't have a whole book, you know).

Perhaps if I had told someone, I would have travelled a different path through life.

But I didn't, so I took the road I'm on – a road where I have experienced this feeling of terror many, many times over the years. And each time I experienced it, I remained silent.

I'm good at silence. I can have a panic attack and you couldn't tell by looking at me. It's not that I'm trying to hide it; it's just that I am entirely unable to speak when it happens.

I am much better than I used to be, but for the first 20 years of my life the terror could literally make me shake for hours. But only if I was alone. If I was *with someone*, for example, in a restaurant, the only parts of me that would shake were the parts hidden beneath the table. As I said, I'm good at silence – even my body cooperates. At least it used to.

Nowadays, my body doesn't cooperate. If you saw me in the supermarket during a terror moment, you could probably tell – something's going on with that lady clutching the shopping trolley. And that's a good thing. It means my body's talking. And talking is better than silence any day of the week.

When I was in college, I met a young man in my philosophy class. He had blue eyes and his parents were from Denmark. I had drawn a picture of a van Gogh painting mentioned in a Heidegger essay the class had been reading. I was showing this to the professor and this young man with blue eyes walked over and looked hard at my drawing. Then he looked at me.

One night we were at an outdoor concert and the terror came to me. I started shaking. He laid next to me on the picnic rug. He didn't know why I was shaking. He just lay beside me, and after a while the shaking stopped.

After a few years, we had two sons, and I was never happier in my life. I had always wanted children, and I knew that had something to do with trying to create a terror-free life for them. They're pretty fearless, so I guess I got that part right.

But my terror never went away.

I had good years and bad years; well, not whole years of course, but the terror always lurked. It still does. And I am still unable to speak while experiencing it. That is one of the reasons I wanted to write this book. To speak out, not just for me, but for all those other people who are good at silence in their own ways and for their own reasons.

This is the road I am presently on: the road somewhere in the middle of this struggle. I do not know where it will lead, but for the first time in my life I can see where the road is heading. It is heading in the direction of learning to talk through my terror of learning to break the silence that I fell into after that first memory. It is not an empty experience, this terror that I feel. It claims a part of me and it has claimed this part since my first memory of me. That is the nature of my struggle. That is all I want to do – to get that part of me back.

Perhaps my struggle is foolish. It's certainly costing me – I don't travel well, I don't do well in restaurants, I don't … well, I have a long list of potential terrorizing experiences. And I'm not 'as much fun' as I used to be, but like I said, it's been a really tough year.

I have never taken antidepressants. I am one of those people who will not take antidepressants. It is not that I am afraid they will 'change' me. It is not the fear of being perceived as morally weak. If there were a pill out there that would help me learn to talk from within the terror, I'd be the first one in the queue when it hit the shelf. But I have read the labels carefully, and 'talking from terror' is not on the list of indications.

I do take benzos to help me get through the terror moments, and there have been plenty in recent years. However, as we mentioned in the medication chapter, benzos will not cure panic.

But I am not looking for a cure.

I am looking for a way to learn to negotiate this road and to find a way to speak. After many dismal starts, I found a therapist who's willing to go along for the ride. And for that I am quite grateful to the universe.

I hope that I can keep my friends and family intact as I continue on this road. But unless I walk it through to the end, I will never reclaim the part of me I lost so long ago. It is not that I'm trying to retrieve something irretrievable. I'm just trying to learn to speak.

I'm good at speaking to strangers these days. In the past few months, just at the onset of terror moments, I've found a way to say a word or two to a stranger standing in a queue or behind a counter. And I will end this story of my struggle with one of my talking-to-strangers stories.

I was in a shop, clutching my tiny bag of apples, and the terror was swooping overhead. A woman in the adjacent queue held roses in her arms. Many, many roses. I turned to her and commented on the number of roses in her arms. She nodded, and said it was a good day.

I turned away, felt the terror threatening again, then turned back to her and asked if it was a good day for her or for someone she knew.

'It's a good day, a great day, for everyone,' she said.

She was oozing the greatness of her day. I could feel it. In fact, I could not turn away from it. I commented on this – the oozing of her greatness – and then she explained the roses.

She'd just flown into Chicago. She was on her way to meet her daughter – a daughter she gave up for adoption. The daughter had phoned her that morning, first time since the adoption, and here she was, in a store, buying roses.

'How old was she when you gave her up for adoption?' I asked.

'When she was born,' the woman answered.

Then she cried, lifting the roses in her arms. There were 56: 28 for each of them, one a piece for each year they had been apart.

Then I cried. I stepped out of my queue and put my arms around her. It was an amazing moment – she with her roses and me with my apples. Just two people in the shop on an ordinary day. Two people meeting on the bumpy road of life.

That's what I try to do these days instead of clutching

shopping trolleys. Terror or not, there's a whole world of people out there and all of them have stories to tell. I am glad that through this book I've been able to tell a little of mine.

Panic diary

Jeanne at age 46

1 February 2004

Dear Diary,

When I was just six years old a classmate vomited on me. I remember it was a sunny spring day and I remember that his name was Paul.

The following day I was afraid to go back to school. My mother tried to comfort me; she promised me that the little boy's mother would surely keep him home in bed that day. So I went to school. And ... you guessed it: Paul was there and he vomited again.

True story.

For years my mother was convinced that all of my anxiety problems stemmed from that single incident. I sort of believed that myself, for a while, anyway.

I had my first panic attack at the age of 7.

I took my first antidepressant at the age of 32.

The 25 years in between were remarkably good for someone who experienced panic attacks on a fairly regular basis. Certainly my life was different, not your average childhood, yet I was part of a close-knit loving family, with parents who tried everything they could think of to help

me. But the fact is, there just wasn't much help available
back then.

So we adapted. My panic attacks were known within my
family as 'my feeling' and, although they limited my life in a lot
of ways, I still managed to be a happy, entertaining child
with a lot of friends.

When I was 12, I went to a sleepover for the first time, even
though I knew I'd be in the loo struggling with 'my feeling' at
some point during the night.

When I was 16 I went to Led Zeppelin and Jethro Tull
concerts fully aware that the jam-packed auditorium would
trigger 'my feeling'.

When I was 19 I started singing with a local rock band in
clubs around the Chicago area. Yes, sometimes the panic
would find me locked in a little lavatory cubicle, but most of
the time I managed.

Then I met the man who would one day become my
husband. It wasn't a 'Hi, how are you' kind of meeting, it was
a thunderbolt, can't-take-my-eyes-off-you kind of meeting.

I was in love. But on our second date I had a panic attack in
a crowded restaurant. My future husband found me outside in
the street, pacing. I told him I was sick; I thought it might be
the fish. He just looked at me for a long time.

A few weeks later we double-dated with a couple of his
friends. And there, in the back seat of this tiny car, I began to
unravel. He reached for my hand.

We never really talked about my disorder, partly because I
didn't know how to. I didn't know what it was, I didn't know it
had a name, or that other people were suffering just like me. I
thought it was 'my feeling'.

We got married and had three kids. The panic came and went.

The year I turned 30 everything changed. Who knows why – maybe because I had three small children. Or maybe because my husband and I were buying a house and starting a small business. Perhaps I had never been subjected to that level of stress before. But suddenly I was having panic attacks every day. I was struggling with obsessive thoughts and impulses that terrified me. My world was shrinking.

With the help of my family doctor I found a good therapist. But the therapy wasn't alleviating any of my symptoms. My husband hung in there, but I knew it was taking a toll on him.

Then my family doctor prescribed the antidepressant imipramine. Within a few weeks my panic stopped. The obsessive thoughts and impulses no longer terrified me and eventually they faded, too. I stopped seeing my therapist, and for a few years things were great, so I went off the imipramine.

Within a year my symptoms returned.

I went back on the imipramine and returned to my therapist. This time we did some serious work together. She opened a door for me and helped me to understand myself as I never had before. I learnt that I needed to monitor my stress levels , the way others might need to monitor their blood sugar. I did a lot of reading and began practising meditation and yoga, something I had made a half-hearted attempt at in years past. I also got serious about an exercise programme.

What I learnt about myself was that regular exercise meant the promise of a good night's sleep. I learnt that yoga and meditation had a calming effect on my mind and resulted in a more positive reaction to the stresses of life.

In 1996, I began to slowly reduce my dose of antidepressant medication. One year later I was off my medication, practicing meditation and yoga as well as exercising on a regular basis.

Yes, I still feel that familiar flutter of panic sometimes. But what I now understand is that that flutter is a part of who I am. Understanding my own fear gave it a whole new color. What works for me are the methods described in this book that are based on the methods by Claire Weekes. But that's just what works for me. You and your doctor should decide what works for you. Just a side note – I still don't leave the house without a Xanax in my bag. I doubt I ever will.

In this brief history of my life, I haven't mentioned my writing, simply because that's another whole story and quite frankly there isn't enough room. I have learnt that, for me, writing is another daily exercise that keeps me mentally well. Whether it's fiction or essays or screenplays or a book on panic attacks, the process of writing brings me joy.

You know, I'm beginning to believe that some form of anxiety or mood disorder is a prerequisite for a career in the arts. Just looking at my small circle of writer and artist friends, I find the number of them who are struggling with anxiety to be suspiciously high. In the words of T. S. Eliot, 'Anxiety is the hand maiden of creativity.'

THE DOCTOR IS IN

In closing, we'd like to reiterate that if you are having panic attacks, first and foremost, you should seek help from a professional. That doesn't mean that the mere presence of anxiety should send you running to a doctor, but if anxiety is interfering with your life, you need to get help.

'Panic is a symptom,' says Dr Mark. 'If you begin changing your behaviour because of your anxiety, then you should see a doctor.'

We asked Dr Charles what the three most important things someone struggling with panic attacks should do: 'Number one is to seek medical or psychological help. Number two is to educate yourself about your illness, and number three is to gain the skills necessary for a sustained remission, such as cognitive-behaviour therapy, meditation or counselling.'

Courage doesn't mean you don't experience fear. Courage is being afraid and doing it anyway.

SOME FINAL FUN FACTS TO AMAZE YOUR FRIENDS

- Roughly half of all those who have panic attacks develop them before the age of 24
- In the United States alone, more than $160 billion is spent annually on mental health disorders, second only to cardiovascular conditions[96]
- 30 per cent of panickers abuse alcohol
- 17 per cent of panickers abuse drugs

ANSWERS

ANSWERS TO THE TWIST ON PAGE 83

F	X	G	O	L	D	D	U	S	T
L	O	I	L	E	U	P	P	T	A
A	P	V	I	E	T	N	A	M	L
S	H	R	V	R	R	H	N	O	M
H	R	U	A	O	A	I	G	O	Q
B	N	S	A	C	U	J	E	L	U
A	H	F	D	S	M	V	R	A	D
C	R	N	S	T	A	R	T	L	E
K	I	O	A	R	L	U	K	T	E
M	U	G	P	A	N	I	C	I	M

ANSWERS TO THE HOKEY-POKEY ON PAGE 129

LWOOFL	FOLLOW
HET	THE
LEWYOL	YELLOW
CIKRB	BRICK
ADOR	ROAD

RECOMMENDED READING

Breggin, Peter R. and Ginger Ross Breggin. *Talking Back to Prozac*. New York: St. Martin's Press, 1994.

Bremner, J. Douglas, MD. *Does Stress Damage the Brain?* New York: W. W. Norton & Company, 2002.

DePaulo, J. R. Jr, MD and L. A. Horvitz. *Understanding Depression*. New York: John Wiley & Sons, 2002.

Figley, Charles R. *Compassion Fatigue*. New York: Brummer/Mazel Psychologial Stress Series, 1995.

Fullerton, C. S. and R. J. Ursano, MD, eds. *Post-Traumatic Stress Disorder*. Washington, DC: American Psychiatric Press, Inc., 1997.

Kramer, Peter, MD. *Listening to Prozac*. New York: Penguin Books, 1997.

Morrison, Andrew L., MD. *The Antidepressant Sourcebook*. New York: Doubleday, 1999.

Penzel, Fred. *Obsessive-Compulsive Disorders*. New York: Oxford Press, 2000.

Shay, Jonathan, MD. *Odysseus in America: Combat Trauma and the Trials of Coming Home*. New York: Scribner, 2002.

Weekes, Claire L., MD. *Hope and Help for Your Nerves*. New York: Penguin Putnam, 1990.

Weinstock, L. and E. Gilman. *Overcoming Panic Disorder*. Lincolnwood, IL: Contemporary Books, 1998.

Wurtzel, Elizabeth. *Prozac Nation*. New York: Houghton Mifflin, 1994.

Yehuda, Rachel, ed. *Treating Trauma Survivors with PTSD*. Washington, DC: American Psychiatric Association, 2002.

ENDNOTES

1 Thomas Barloon and Russel Noyes, 'Did Darwin Have Panic Disorder?' in *The Journal of the American Medical Association, 27* Jan 1997, 138–41.

2 Robert Spitzer, *Diagnostic and Statistical Manual of Mental Disorders (DSM-IV-TR)*, 4th ed. (Washington, DC: American Psychiatric Association, 2000), 436.

3 Lorna Weinstock and Eleanor Gilman, *Overcoming Panic Disorder* (Lincolnwood, IL: Contemporary Books, 1998), 213.

4 Ibid., 212.

5 *Thornton's Wildness*. www.uk.news/interview. 4 Feb 2002.

6 Alix Spiegel, 'The Man Behind Psychiatry's Diagnostic Manual' in *All Things Considered*, 18 Aug 2003. National Public Radio broadcast.

7 Ibid.

8 *DSM-IV-TR*, 393–4.

9 Jennet Conant, 'Winona Ryder: Mining Her Memories to Play a Troubled Soul' in *New York Times*, 14 Nov 1999.

10 R. Plomin and G. E. McClearn, eds. *Nature, Nurture, and Psychology* (Washington, DC: American Psychological Association Press, 1993), 269–84.

11 Edmund J. Bourne, *The Anxiety and Phobia Workbook* (Oakland, CA: New Harbinger Pub, 1995), 24.

12 *DSM-IV-TR*.

13 Lorna Weinstock and Eleanor Gilman, *Overcoming Panic Disorder* (Lincolnwood, IL: Contemporary Books, 1998).

14 American Psychiatric Association, *Statement of Diagnosis & Treatment Disorders*, Release No. 03-39, 25 Sept 2003.

[15] National Institute of Mental Health panic statistics.

[16] Lorna Weinstock and Eleanor Gilman, *Overcoming Panic Disorder* (Lincolnwood, IL: Contemporary Books, 1998), xiii.

[17] David Satcher, MD, 'Mental Health: A Report of the Surgeon General' *Surgeon General's Report* (Washington, DC: U.S. Public Health Service, 1999).

[18] Edmund J. Bourne, *The Anxiety and Phobia Workbook* (Oakland, CA: New Harbinger Pub, 1995), 8–9.

[19] A. Ravelli, R. V. Bihl and G. Van Zessen, 'Results of the Netherlands Mental Health Survey and Incidence Study (NEMESIS)' in *Journal of Psychiatry*, 9, 1998, 531–44.

[20] *Statistics and Facts Sheet* (Silver Springs, MD: Anxiety Disorders Association of America, 2002).

[21] Nicola Christie, 'Woody Allen on Woody Allen' in *Reuter's*, 29 Aug 2003.

[22] Steven Phillipson, *Center for Cognitive Behavior Psychotherapy* (New York: 2003).

[23] *DSM-IV-TR*, 458.

[24] Obsessive-Compulsive Disorder at JHU, *The Hope For Tomorrow* (Baltimore, MD: Johns Hopkins University, 2002).

[25] *DSM-IV-TR*, 457.

[26] Claire L.Weekes, MD, *Hope and Help for Your Nerves* (New York: Penguin Putnam, 1990).

[27] Steven Phillipson, *Center for Cognitive Behavior Psychotherapy* (New York: 2003).

[28] *DSM-IV-TR*, 461.

[29] Mary Lynn Hendrix and Margaret Stock, NIMH Publication Number 99-3755 (Boston, MA, Nov 2002).

[30] Fred Penzel, *Obsessive-Compulsive Disorders* (New York: Oxford Press, 2000), 2.

[31] National Institute of Mental Health, *Facts About Social Phobia*, NIMH Publication Number OM-99-4171 Revised, 2003.

[32] *DSM-IV-TR*, 393.

[33] National Institute of Mental Health, *Facts About Social Phobia*, NIMH Publication Number OM-99-4171 Revised, 2003.

[34] Willard Waller, *The Veteran Comes Back* (New York: Dryden, 1944), 109.

[35] Charles R. Figley, *Compassion Fatigue* (New York: Brunner/Mazel Publishers, 1995), xiii.

[36] John P. Wilson, Matthew J. Friedman and Jacob D. Linday, eds. *Treating Psychological Trauma and PTSD* (New York: The Guilford Press, 2001), 5.

[37] Rachel Yehuda, ed., *Treating Trauma Survivors with PTSD* (Washington, DC: American Psychiatric Association, 2002), 24. Also see 'Post-Traumatic Stress Disorder in the National Comorbidity Survey', R. C. Kessler, A. Sonnega, E. Bromet et al. In *Archives of General Psychiatry* 52, 1995, 1048–60.

[38] Jonathan Shay, MD, *Odysseus in America: Combat Trauma and the Trials of Coming Home* (New York: Scribner, 2002).

[39] Rachel Yehuda, ed., 'The National Vietnam Veterans Readjustment Study (NVVRS)' in *Treating Trauma Survivors with PTSD* (Washington, DC: American Psychiatric Association, 2002), 25.

[40] Charles Figley, *Compassion Fatigue* (New York: Brunner/Mazel Publishers, 1995), xiii.

[41] John P. Wilson, Matthew J. Friedman and Jacob D. Linday, eds. *Treating Psychological Trauma and PTSD* (New York: The Guilford Press, 2001), 6.

[42] *DSM-IV-TR*, 463.

[43] Ibid., 463.

[44] John P. Wilson, Matthew J. Friedman and Jacob D. Linday, eds. *Treating Psychological Trauma and PTSD* (New York: The Guilford Press, 2001), 25.

[45] Rachel Yehuda, ed., *Treating Trauma Survivors with PTSD* (Washington, DC: American Psychiatric Association, 2002), 77.

[46] B. D. Grinage, 'Diagnosis and Management of Post-Traumatic Stress Disorder' in *American Family Physician*, 15 Dec 2003, 68(12), 2401–8.

[47] Carol S. Fullerton and Robert J. Ursano, MD, eds. *Post-Traumatic Stress Disorder* (Washington, DC: American Psychiatric Press, Inc., 1997), 225.

[48] Ibid.

[49] Ibid.

[50] Christopher Snowbeck, 'Health' on Post-gazette.com (Pittsburgh, PA, 7 Jan 2004).

[51] J. Raymond DePaulo, Jr., MD and Leslie Alan Horvitz, *Understanding Depression* (New York: John Wiley & Sons, 2002), 17.

[52] *DSM-IV-TR*, 327.

[53] Michael C. Miller, MD, 'Going Beyond Prozac' in *Newsweek*, Dec 8, 2003, 69.

[54] J. Raymond DePaulo, Jr., MD and Leslie Alan Horvitz, *Understanding Depression* (New York: John Wiley & Sons, 2002), 26.

[55] Mitzi Waltz, *Adult Bipolar Disorders* (Sebastopol, CA: O'Reilly & Associates, 2002), 91.

[56] Rob Nagel, *SAD: More Than Just the Winter Blues* (Farmington Hills, MI, 2000).

[57] J. Raymond DePaulo, Jr., MD and Leslie Alan Horvitz, *Understanding Depression* (New York: John Wiley & Sons, 2002), 216.

[58] Michael C. Miller, MD, 'How Genes Affect Moods' in *Newsweek* 8 Dec 2003, 70.

[59] J. Raymond DePaulo, Jr, MD and Leslie Alan Horvitz, *Understanding Depression* (New York: John Wiley & Sons, 2002), 38.

[60] 'Panic Disorder'. Warner Bros. Entertainment. www.extratv.warnerbros.com. 7 Jan 2000.

[61] Andrew L. Morrison, MD, *The Antidepressant Source Book* (New York: Doubleday, 1999), 13.

[62] Ibid., 14.

[63] Jacqueline Krohn and Frances Taylor, *Finding the Right Treatment* (Point Roberts, WA: Hartley and Marks, 1999), 409.

[64] Ada P. Kahn and Ronald M. Doctor, *Facing Fears* (New York: Checkmark Books, 2000), 116.

[65] Lynne Freeman, *Panic Free* (Colorado Springs, CO: Piccadilly Books, 1998), 155.

[66] Andrew L. Morrison, MD, *The Antidepressant Source Book* (New York, Doubleday, 1999), 7.

[67] Jacqueline Krohn and Frances Taylor, *Finding the Right Treatment* (Point Roberts, WA: Hartley and Marks, 1999), 409.

[68] Ann Garris Goiser, Review of *Valley of the Dolls* in *America's Book Review* online www.bookpage.com, 1997.

[69] *Webster's New Twentieth Century Dictionary*, 2nd ed. (New York: Simon & Schuster, 1983).

[70] Lorna Weinstock and Eleanor Gilman, *Overcoming Panic Disorder* (Lincolnwood, IL: Contemporary Books, 1998), 142.

[71] Albert Ellis, 'Rational-Emotive Behavior Therapy (REBT)' on www.rebt.org (New York: Albert Ellis Institute, 2000).

[72] Lorna Weinstock and Eleanor Gilman, *Overcoming Panic Disorder* (Lincolnwood, IL: Contemporary Books, 1998), 228.

[73] National Institutes of Mental Health, *Understanding Panic Disorder*, NIH Publication Number 95-3509 Revised, 1995.

[74] Ibid. Also see Lorna Weinstock and Eleanor Gilman, *Overcoming Panic Disorder* (Lincolnwood, IL: Contemporary Books 1998), 142.

[75] Ibid., 188–90.

[76] ScientificAmerican.com. 17 July 2001.

[77] Kate Murphy, 'There's Entrancing News About Hypnosis' in *Business Week*, 2 Feb 2004, 88.

[78] American Society of Clinical Hypnosis, 'Information for the General Public' Fact Sheet. www.asch.net/genpubinfo.htm.

79 Terence M. Keane, 'The Role of Exposure Therapy in the Psychological Treatment of PTSD' in *NCP Clinical Quarterly* 5 (4), Fall 1995.

80 *VR Therapy for Spider Phobia*. (Seattle, WA: Human Interface Technology Laboratory) www.hitl.washington.edu/projects/exposure.

81 Francine Shapiro, *EMDR as an Integrative Psychotherapy Approach: Experts of Diverse Orientations Explore the Paradigm Prism* (Washington, DC: American Psychological Association Books, 2002).

82 Robert Stickgold, MD, 'EMDR: A Putative Neruobiological Mechanism of Action' in *Journal of Clinical Psychology* 58 (1), 69.

83 Edmund J. Bourne, *The Anxiety and Phobia Workbook* (Oakland, CA: New Harbinger Pub, 1995), 78.

84 Ibid., 79.

85 Lorna Weinstock and Eleanor Gilman, *Overcoming Panic Disorder* (Lincolnwood, IL: Contemporary Books, 1998), 136.

86 Jacqueline Krohn and Frances Taylor, *Finding the Right Treatment* (Point Roberts, WA: Hartley and Marks, 1999), 225.

87 Howard Kent, *Yoga Made Easy* (Allentown, PA: Quarto, 1993), 10.

88 Ibid.

89 Ibid., 9.

90 Jacqueline Krohn and Frances Taylor, *Finding the Right Treatment* (Point Roberts, WA: Hartley and Marks, 1999), 87.

91 Ada P. Kahn and Ronald M. Doctor, *Facing Fears* (New York: Checkmark Books, 2000), 261.

92 Edmund J. Bourne, *The Anxiety and Phobia Workbook* (Oakland, CA: New Harbinger Pub, 1995), 91–2.

93 Lynne Freeman, *Panic Free* (Colorado Springs: Heathwise Publishers, 1998), 51.

94 Ibid., 54.

95 Ibid., 56.

96 American Psychiatric Association, *Statement of Diagnosis & Treatment Disorders*, 2, Sept 2003.

INDEX

Executive Editor Brenda Rosen
Managing Editor Clare Churly
Executive Art Editor Sally Bond
Designer Nigel Soper
Production Controller Aileen O'Reilly